LINCOI
AND THE HUMAN INTEREST STORIES OF
THE GETTYSBURG NATIONAL CEMETERY

WHEN YOU GO HOME
TELL THEM OF US AND SAY,
FOR THEIR TOMORROW
WE GAVE OUR TODAY.

By
James M. Cole
Rev. Roy E. Frampton

Dedication

We dedicate this book to our mothers

Catherine Codori Cole, whose great grand father had Pickett's Charge rudely transit his farm fields in 1863 and to Eva Frampton Gallagher.

Their support of this project and faith in us has never flagged. Thank God, for the gift, in this life, of these two mothers filled with the spirit of gentleness and love.

Acknowledgments

Many individuals and institutions have contributed to the research and writing of this book. Sincere gratitude is given to Sue Kerrigan and Edward Guy who under a rigid task-master, assisted in researching the military files of many soldiers. Thanks also to Louise Arnold Friend, William Bowling, Patricia Cole O'Brien and Dave Weaver for their labor at proof-reading and editing the manuscript. The personal cooperation of Kathy George, Eric Campball, Tim Smith, and other staff members of the National Park Service and Battlefield Guides of Gettysburg is greatly appreciated. Also the staffs of the National Archives and U.S. Army Military History Institute at Carlisle, especially Michael J. Winey and Randy Hackenburg of the Photographic Division at USAMHI should receive high praise.

Many others made important contributions, such as Woody Christ, Dave Friend, Kenneth Cole, William Ridinger, and William Cole. I would also wish to express my heart-felt appreciation to my two wonderful children, Eddie and Heather Frampton for their patience, understanding and support in this Cemetery project.

Printed in the United States of America by The Sheridan Press, Hanover, Pennsylvania.

CONTENTS

Part II

The aftermath of the Battle of Gettysburg
(National Archives)

Introduction

This is the story of Abraham Lincoln and the men of The Gettysburg National Cemetery.

The purpose of this history is to explain how Gettysburg came to be the nation's first national cemetery, how President Lincoln came to be involved and why his Gettysburg Address became a new political revolution transforming the Union into "a new nation."

Emphasis is also given to those events in Lincoln's life that preceded Gettysburg and give a relevant background to that historic moment. Lincoln's greatest words from other speeches and writings are also excerpted to demonstrate how he became a lord of language and why those words will live in classic greatness.

Numerous photographs and individual stories of the men and the events described are also included—many of which are published for the first time.

So this is their story, the story of the boys of the Blue and Gray, the known and unknown who preserved and passed on to us a rich history and heritage that we now call our own.

Temporary Grave and Headmarkers—
Following the battle, temporary massed graves were dug for the dead of both armies. Temporary headboards (as seen left) were placed and inscribed or cut upon to maintain identities. The efforts were often quickly and crudely done and soon faded in the elements or lost. Of the 3,512 reported to have been reburied in the National Cemetery a third could not be identified and thus classified as unknown.

The Great Battle

It was the second year of the war that General Robert E. Lee led his powerful army north to the gently rolling farm fields of Southern Pennsylvania. Soon, the land would come to know the terrible torment of war.

Here, during those first three days of July 1863, Lee's 75,000 man army met the 97,000 man army of General George G. Meade in the greatest battle of the War. Never before had such a spectacle been seen on the North American Continent: Hundreds of booming cannons proclaiming their death and destruction, drums and bugles and bright battle flags leading thousands into magnificent charges. Charges that were beautiful, majestic, and terrible! One

Confederate assault that would crash against the Union infantry and artillery massed upon Cemetery Ridge—an assault that would result in a loss of half of the 12,000 participants and would win enduring fame as ''Pickett's Charge.''

With the failure of the Charge, the epic battle was over the Union saved. And although the war would rage for two more terrible years, the Confederacy would never recover. And through the deepening twilight of Confederate military power all who had been there, would remember.

Of the 172,000 combatants, 51,000 became casualties in a four year war that appallingly caused the death of 600,000 men—America's greatest national tragedy.

The temporary wooden grave marker and photograph of Lieut. F.C. Goodrich of the 2nd United States Infantry. It is one of the few known to exist from the initial markers that identified soldiers buried on the battlefield and at hospital sites prior to their exhumation and re-burial in the Soldiers' Cemetery.
(Special thanks to Peter Monahan and Andrew Larson of Lee's Headquarters Museum Gettysburg where this rare relic is on permanent display.)

Andrew Curtin—The energetic Governor of Pennsylvania was one of those responsible for the eventual establishment of the Gettysburg National Cemetery. (NPS)

David Wills—This thirty-two year old Gettysburg attorney was Governor Curtin's agent and tirelessly labored for the concept of a National Cemetery at Gettysburg. (LC)

Aftermath of Battle

Seldom does a town the size of Gettysburg find itself in such circumstances as those created by the enormous conflict. It has been said that as theater replaces life, so too does nostalgia replace history. This is particularly true with the realities of war. Although the exhausted regiments began to retire from the field of battle on the fourth of July, the magnitude of what had occurred did not become apparent until the armies had departed. Gone were the bugles and bright battle flags. Instead, the air was now pierced with the sounds of dying men, the bitter sobbing of the permanently crippled and the terrifying cries of the delirious. In place of the youthful soldiers, so full of life, there were now the mangled forms of the dead.

We tend to be content with the fragments of history. We read of battles and armies and yet only comprehend a bloodless, painless and ungraspable abstraction of an unreal past.

We do, however, relate far better to the events experienced by the individual in history. Because of that, we will attempt to portray the true meaning of this history through the eyes, and words, of individuals whose fate it was to be caught up in the events that occurred in those terrible days of 1863. This history, or, more precisely, these human events should neither be romanticized nor forgotten.

Following the battle torrential rains added to the difficulty. One volunteer nurse, a member of the Sisters of Charity wrote of her journey: "The rains had filled the roads with water, and here it was red with blood. Our horses could hardly be forced to proceed with the horrid objects before them, the very carriage wheels rolling through blood."

Another observer to the aftermath of battle was J. Howard Wert, a citizen of Gettysburg who witnessed the horrors at Saint Francis Xavier church and wrote

"There were gruesome sights all around. The sacred edifice was filled with suffering humanity. Groans and shrieks and cries of agony rent the air. In the little yard of the church stood the amputating tables and the surgeons at them, bedabbled with blood were ceaseless in their work, whilst legs and arms deftly cut off were being thrown upon an increasing pile."

Another, The Rev. Leonard Gardner from nearby York Springs wrote that, "Some were hurt in such a way that they could not turn their bodies from the time they had laid there. Others were compelled to die in their blood and filth without power to relieve themselves."

Miss Sallie Ann Myers, a Gettysburg teacher, recorded this in her diary, "I went into the Roman Catholic Church. The men were scattered all over it, some lying in the pews and some on the bare floor. The suffering and groans of the wounded and dying were terrible to see and hear. I knelt by the first one inside the door and said: 'What can I do for you?' He looked up at me with mournful, fearless eyes and said: 'Nothing, I am going to die.' To be met thus by the first one I addressed was more than my overwrought nerves could bear and I went hastily out, sat down on the church step and cried.''

Volunteer nurses came from considerable distances to assist with the massive task of caring for the wounded among the 51,000 casualties. One touching report of a Philadelphia woman related her experience with a Confederate amputee. The newly arrived woman was asked if she was willing to ''wash a rebel prisoner.'' Her reply was prompt: ''Certainly, I have a son in the Union Army and I would like to have somebody wash him.'' The official report of the New York State Commission on the Wounded continued: ''With towels and water in a tin basin, she cheerfully walked through the mud to the tent, careful not to disturb his amputated leg. She gently removed the old shirt and began to wash him, but the tenderness of a mother's heart was at work, and she began to cry over him saying that she imagined she was washing her own son. This was more than he could bear. He too, began to weep and ask God to bless her for her kindness to him. The scene was too much for the bystanders and they left the northern mother and the southern son to their sacred grief.''

The United Presbyterian Church stood some distance from the street and had a fence enclosing the surrounding grounds. Here, two long trenches were dug, the dead were wrapped in army blankets and buried as close together as they could be placed. In the report ''The Care of the Wounded after the Battle of Gettysburg,'' it states, ''Before these trenches were filled up with ground, rain fell and it was necessary to lay heavy boards over the bodies to keep them down and in place.''

With the magnitude of the conflict, 113 improvised hospitals sprang up. Every church, school and public building was used to house the thousands of wounded and dying.

Following the swift departure of the armies, some of the dead would remain unburied for days. Even some of the hastily buried had their graves rudely opened as Gettysburg's accessibility in the North allowed families a chance to locate a deceased loved one. (Since no system of military identification existed prior to World War I, over half of the battle dead would become at least partially unknown.)

A National Cemetery is Conceived

During the American Civil War no practical national system existed for the proper burial of Civil War dead. Usually, the deceased were hastily buried where killed to quickly become a nameless grave and a remembrance in only the hearts of a few.

On February 28, 1862, however, the Pennsylvania Legislature passed an act which provided for the care of her wounded and the burial of her battle dead. With the intent to carry out the law, Pennsylvania's Governor, Andrew Curtain, soon appeared on the scene.

Appalled by the sufferings of the wounded, he appointed a Gettysburg attorney, David Wills, as his agent to alleviate the suffering and to assist in the effort to bury the dead. Thirty-two years old, the energetic Wills would become the main force in the eventual establishment of the Gettysburg National Cemetery.

In his first report, on July 24, 1863, Wills emphasized the poor condition of the temporary graves. As an example, he noted how some of the shallow graves had eroded away by the heavy July rains exposing the decaying bodies. On July 28th, Gettysburg's Adams Sentinel newspaper reported that, ''Governor Curtain has made arrangements with David Wills, Esq. of this place for the removal of all Pennsylvanians killed in the late battles, furnishing transportation for the body and one attendant at the expense of the State.'' One undertaker reported that up to seven hundred bodies were thus transported in July in pine coffins to their families. At this point, however, the burial detail protested their oppressive working conditions. Not only was their fear of pestilence, there also existed a suffocating stench of the decaying bodies amidst the heat and humidity of July. The five thousand dead horse carcasses would also not be completely burned and buried for several weeks. Finally, by the end of July, the military ordered a cessation in the movement of any more bodies.

As the exhumation of the bodies ceased, Wills conceived of a plan to have the remaining dead buried in Gettysburg's local Evergreen Cemetery. He gained no support for this idea so then he proposed a plan for a joint civilian-military cemetery which was also rejected. Eventually, a third concept was adopted as he explained later that, ''All were of the decided opinion that the Soldiers' Cemetery should be made an independent cemetery, and the control and management of it retained by the States interested.''

Less than a year later, on March 25, 1864, Governor Curtain signed into law the Act of Incorporation establishing the Soldiers' National Cemetery with a governing board of commissioners from the states involved.

Entrance to the Evergreen Cemetery—Built in 1855, two years after the establishment of the town cemetery. Union General Meade first conferred with some of his generals at this gate house upon arrival on the battlefield. The local cemetery association failed in its efforts to sell lots to the states for the burial of their dead. (LC)

Exhumation of the Dead—Pictured here (front right) is Samuel Weaver, Superintendent of Exhumation, who personally witnessed every exhumation until reinterments to the cemetery were completed in March of 1864. The Weaver family were also photographers from the nearby town of Hanover, Pa. and were the photographers who took the rare photographs of the cemetery dedication on November 19th. Note the burial detail. All of the actual exhumations were done by hired black laborers. This photograph was taken in Hanover, 16 miles from Gettysburg and attests to the epic scale of the terrain covered by the combatants. (Hanover Historical Society)

Thus did the cemetery assume a national character involving the States. With the animosity engendered by the war, however, no consideration was given to the creation of a cemetery for the burial of the battle dead of the Confederacy. Instead, their bodies would remain in massed graves upon the battlegrounds until removed by the Ladies Memorial Association of the South in 1872. These post-war reinternments were made in the southern cities of Richmond, Charleston, Savannah and Raleigh.

The Cemetery Plan

With the approval of Governor Curtain and all of the other seventeen states involved. Wills then purchased, in the name of Pennsylvania, 17 acres of Cemetery Hill for $2,475.87 and had preliminary plans for internment drawn up. A contract was also granted for the reburial of each soldier for $1.59 per body.

The grounds were not only on the main Union battle lines and visually attractive with the hill's elevation but it would also be located adjacent the town cemetery, a concept closely resembling what the states had originally rejected. Wills planned to have the dead buried at random as they were re-interred to the cemetery, but the State of Massachusetts opposed this, resulting in the final plan to grant each state its own separate plot.

This final plan would contain an unforeseen flaw, however. In the reburials, thirty soldiers could be identified by name but not by state and would then suffer the fate of having to lose their identity by being interred in the section of Unknown.

Wills' purchase of the 17 acre site for the cemetery was only "after much difficulty" and consisted of five different lots and resulting in an elongated or boot-shaped pattern. Because of the unusual shape of the combined odd lots, William Saunders, the landscape architect (and founder of the American farmers organization, the Grange) hired for the layout, was forced to adopt a unique semicircular pattern of graves to fit this boot-shaped pattern.

On, August 17th, Wills reported to Governor Curtain that the chief executives of fifteen of the other seventeen states had pledged their support for the cemetery plan and concluded by writing:

> I think it would be showing only a proper respect for the health of this community not to commence the exhuming of the dead, and removal to the Cemetery until the month of November, and in the meantime the ground should be artistically laid out, and consecrated by appropriate ceremonies.[3]

Thus the reinterments to the Cemetery would not begin until the fall of 1863 and continue into 1864. When the exhumations began on October 23rd the burial detail was required to follow a rigid system of identification and inventory. Samuel Weaver, the Superintendent of Exhumations, reported that no grave was permitted to be opened or a body searched unless he was present. Weaver in his report stated:

> I was inflexible in enforcing this rule, and here can say, with the greatest satisfaction to myself and to the friends of the soldiers, that I saw every body taken out of its temporary resting place, and all the pockets carefully searched; and where the grave was not marked, I examined all the clothing and everything about the body to find the name.[4]

Although it was known that the chronic shortage of uniforms caused southern soldiers to wear confiscated northern clothing, Weaver said that the "rebel underclothing" of cotton was "infallible" in determining whether the deceased was Union or Confederate.

David Wills said of Weaver that, "through his untiring and faithful efforts the bodies in many unmarked graves" were identified, "sometimes by letters, by papers, receipts, certificates, diaries, memorandum books, photographs, marks on the clothing, belts, or cartridge boxes."[5]

The burials were made in long semi-circular trenches dug to a depth of three feet and in wood coffins supplied by the Quartermaster General of the army. Then, temporary headboards with an assigned number were placed at each grave with the aforementioned information. Of the 3,512 reported to have been reburied in the National Cemetery, 979 were completely unknown and 1,664 were partially unknown. Interestingly, all of the coffins were laid with the heads of the deceased facing the center of the semi-circle where, today, the Soldiers' National Monument, with Liberty atop, faces them in silent tribute.

Regarding Wills' suggestion about consecration, Curtain replied on August 31st stating:

> The proper consecration of the grounds must claim our early attention and, as soon as we can do so, our fellow purchasers should be invited to join us in the performance of suitable ceremonies on the occasion.[6]

Edward Everett

By September 23rd a date for the dedication had been set and the eighteen states unanimously selected as its main speaker, Edward Everett, America's foremost orator.

Everett replied to the committee's invitation on September 26th stating that the proposed date of dedication, October 23rd, was not suitable and pleaded for a month's postponement writing, "I cannot safely name an earlier time than the 19th of November."[7] So prominent was the stature and reputation of the 69 year old Bostonian that his request was immediately accepted and the specific date of dedication would thus be determined by him.

The planned content of the Everett address was also revealed in his letter when he wrote "It will demand as full a narrative of the events of the three important days as the

Edward Everett—America's foremost orator whose fate was to be on the same platform with Lincoln. Over the decades authors would unjustly malign Everett's Gettysburg speech in order to enhance the fame of the Lincoln address. The greatness of Lincoln's Address, however needs no comparative reinforcement, its greatness is self-evident and stands on its own merits. (NPS)

limits of the hour will admit, and some appropriate discussion of the political character of the great struggle, of which The Battle of Gettysburg is one of the most momentous incidents."[8]

Who was Edward Everett? Although a relatively unknown historical figure today, in 1863 his fame was widespread. Born in 1794, he would graduate from Harvard University with the highest honors at age 18 and become a Unitarian minister, member of the U.S. House of Representatives, Governor of Massachusetts, U.S. Minister to Great Britain, President of Harvard, U.S. Senator and Secretary of State. In 1860 he accepted the call of the Constitutional Union Party and ran as its vice-presidential candidate losing to the newly established Republican Party and its first successful presidential candidate, Abraham Lincoln.

Regarded as the oratorical successor to the famed statesman Daniel Webster, Everett had been tirelessly traveling throughout the northern States delivering his pro-Lincoln war lecture, The Causes and Conduct of the War. Prior to the War he was nationally famous for a two hour oration on George Washington that was presented to large audiences on 134 occasions. Earnings from these ornate addresses approached $100,000.

President Abraham Lincoln—This photograph was taken by Alexander Gardner November 15th, three days before Lincoln traveled to Gettysburg. (LC)

The Lincoln Invitation

By early November, with the ceremony less than three weeks away, no national governmental nor military official had been consulted on the arrangements. Apparently, no consideration had been given to inviting federal participation in the ceremony. Perhaps many assumed that the government officials—particularly the President—would not consider a distant cemetery dedication with the demands of the ongoing War and as the armies remained poised for battle in the South.

Nonetheless, and apparently as an afterthought, on November 2nd David Wills wrote to President Lincoln saying, "I am authorized by the governors of the different States to invite you to be present, and to participate in these ceremonies, which will doubtless be very imposing and solemnly impressive. It is the desire that, after the oration, you, as Chief Executive of the nation, formally set apart these grounds to their sacred use by a few appropriate remarks."[9]

The Wills invitation is of importance in two respects: First, the President was indirectly informed that he would not be the main orator. Secondly, he would be expected to undertake a minor role through, "a few appropriate remarks." Undoubtedly, the respective roles assigned to

Everett and Lincoln stemmed from Everett's aforementioned national oratorical reputation in a formal setting. Only later with the Gettysburg Address and, to a lesser extent Lincoln's Second Inaugural Address, would the Lincoln oratory win fame in its own right. The unpopular nature of the War and the repeated military disasters in the South had negatively affected the President's popularity. Most certainly, the modern day fame and memory of the martyred President did not exist in 1863.

Following the Lincoln invitation, Wills also extended a belated invitation to Lincoln's Cabinet and informally invited the President, Mr. Everett and Governor Curtain to be his house guests at his Gettysburg residence. By November 9th, he had accepted the invitation and within a short ten days one of the world's greatest speeches in the modern English language would be written.

The night that Lincoln accepted his Gettysburg invitation he journeyed across town to, "the performance at Ford's Theater and sat in the box he regularly occupied in the second tier to the right, a curtained hideaway of lush red satin and brocade-perfect for reflecting on a cemetery while the eyes were watching the stage. That night John Wilkes Booth was playing in The Marble Heart."[10]

The Lincoln Legends

It is indeed regrettable that the nation's finest oration would come to be associated with a variety of myth, legend and untruth. No single episode of Lincoln's life presents more controversy and divergent opinion than the writing and presentation of his Gettysburg masterpiece.

Most of the contradictory testimony came from faulty memories recalling events up to fifty years after their occurrence. Additionally, two similar ceremonies occurred in the Cemetery shortly after its dedication. These were the laying of the cornerstone of the Soldiers Monument in the Cemetery in 1865 and its subsequent dedication in 1869. What is certain is that how Lincoln came to write the Address, when he wrote it and how would be received remains in dispute.

John G. Nicolay, Lincoln's personal secretary, would later write in Century Magazine: "There is no decisive record of when Mr. Lincoln wrote the first sentences of his proposed address. He probably followed his usual habit in such matters, using great deliberation in arranging his thoughts and moulding his phrases mentally, waiting to reduce them to writing until they had taken satisfactory form."[11]

Three witnesses have stated that Lincoln showed the Gettysburg Address to them in Washington prior to his Gettysburg journey. Simon Cameron, Lincoln's former Secretary of War, stated: "Mr. Lincoln wrote that speech in the White House several days before he went to Gettysburg. He took great pains in writing it. On a visit to him he showed it to me. It was written with a lead pencil on commercial note paper."[12]

Lincoln's Gettysburg Journey

Lincoln began his Gettysburg journey by a special four car train by way of Baltimore at noon on November 18th.

Over the years, various authors have claimed that Lincoln wrote the Gettysburg Address during the journey. The most famous version of the Lincoln legend is the Mary Shipman Andrews story, "The Perfect Tribute," published in 1906. Describing Lincoln's train journey she wrote:

> "He glanced about inquiringly—there was nothing to write upon. Across the car the Secretary of State had just opened a package of books and their wrapping of brown paper lay on the floor, torn carelessly in a zig-zag. The President stretched a long arm. 'Mr. Seward, may I have this to do a little writing?' . . . he labored as the hours flew, building together close fitted word on word, sentence on sentence."[13]

Nothing could be further from fact. Although it is true that eyewitnesses observed Lincoln writing on the moving train, none ever claimed that it was the Gettysburg Address. Instead, every known witness aboard the train merely assumed that this was what they had observed. As an example, the first page of the first of five copies of the Address from Lincoln's own band is written on Executive Mansion Stationery, suggesting that its source, the White House, was also the site of its use. Secondly, the penmanship is of such firm quality that it bears none of the jerkiness of the one known document authored by Lincoln on a train, his Farewell Speech at Springfield, Illinois of 1861.

The evidence of a lapse in time and place of authorship of the Address is also suggested by the fact that the white letterhead paper of the first page is written in ink while the second page is written with a lead pencil upon large sized lined legal paper. Thus the first page was probably written in Washington, the second, at Gettysburg in the home of David Wills the night before and morning of its presentation.

Nonetheless, it is regrettable that the nation's finest oration is almost universally believed to have been belatedly and hurriedly scribbled upon a discarded piece of brown wrapping paper.

After the six hour journey, the train, filled with the weary press—governmental, diplomatic and military travelers finally rumbled to a stop in Gettysburg at dusk. Here, the President was greeted by his host David Wills, General Darius Couch, the senior army officer of the region's Department of the Susquehanna, and Edward Everett. From the train station the entourage made its way through the immense crowd with some difficulty walking one block South to the Will's home, the most imposing private residence at the very center of the town. They had arrived in a town in which no one was ready for their rendezvous with history. The President had not completed his speech, the town was not ready to handle the thousands racing to the scene and the only available access for many to the town,

the Northern Central Railroad, was in its management of the transportation system described in this fashion by the New York World: "Not one backwoods Methodist Camp meeting in a hundred but is better managed."

Not all of the dignitaries would successfully arrive for the next day's event however. In a vain attempt to attend, Alexander Ramsey, The Governor of Minnesota, left the state capital of St. Paul on November 12th and travelled east by way of boat and train. "By 4:30 a.m. on the 18th he had made his way to Pittsburgh where he manfully boarded the mail train for Harrisburg. He arrived there at 5:00 p.m." Then, continuing south and into November 19th, the day of dedication, he arrived at a point fifteen miles east of Gettysburg and, "stranded at Hanover Junction in the wee small hours, he would abandon the idea of attending the ceremonies."[14]

Eve of Dedication

As Governor Ramsey was on his futile expedition, others too found the train transport system woefully inadequate. The correspondent of the Cincinnati Commercial complained that, "there are no railroads in the United States that comprise so many discomforts, delays, vexations, and privations to the passengers, or exhibit so mean and illiberal a spirit as the Northern Central and its legitimate offspring, the Gettysburg Branch."[15]

Aboard another special train from Harrisburg were Governor Curtain, three generals, and the Governors of Ohio, West Virginia, New York, and Indiana. Also aboard was Berry R. Sulgrove, editor of the Indianapolis Journal, who recorded his ultimate disgust with the events that transpired that night: "Our excursion from Harrisburg was certainly the worst conceived, arranged and executed expedition of the war not excepting the Peninsula campaign. We started at two o'clock and got away at five. We ran fifteen miles, and the engine . . . broke away from the tender and tore the water pipes of the tank in two. That compelled us to wait till another engine could come from Harrisburg . . . By the time the new engine reached us it was dark, and everybody was hungry . . . Some of the party had furnished a 'lunch,' but just as we were about to eat, the lamps were taken out, and . . . it was impossible to pick out anything . . . and so we went hungry . . . About every ten miles we ran back three to see how far we had got, or if there was any way to keep from getting further . . . Grumbling became almost mutiny. Governor Cameron, who owns the road, was freely advised that if he wanted to run for President he had better not let anybody into the convention who was in that car."[16]

Finally, at 11:00 p.m. the train rattled to a stop at the Gettysburg depot where Curtain and his guests walked the one block south to the Wills house.

Here they found a town that one said "was in chaos over the new invasion." Large boisterous crowds had formed in the town as many, literally, had no place to go. A Baltimore

The Gettysburg Railway Station—Built in 1858, it was here where President Lincoln and the other dignitaries would arrive the night before his immortal address. The train station is preserved today exactly as it was in 1863. (Lane Studio, Gettysburg)

reporter described the throng as being composed of: "State, county and city officials, Governors, Legislators, municipal fathers and other civic functionaries, statesmen, philosophers, poets, editors, men of science, artizens, mechanics, tillers of the soil and navigators of the seas."[17] Also on the scene was a full regiment of infantry from Baltimore as well as a squadron of calvary and two batteries of artillery.

Wills would have thirty-eight guests at his home that night of November 18th. He entertained those distinguished visitors with a dinner party and a reception. The Wills home was one of the first three story structures built in south-central Pennsylvania and the second floor room occupied by the President had a window that overlooked the intersection where the ten highways of the region converged and that had originally drawn the two armies to their mortal combat.

Wills, an attorney as Lincoln once was, had studied under Thaddeus Stevens whose former law office was visable from Lincoln's room. Stevens was now a U.S. Congressman from Pennsylvania. His powerful oratorical skills had now propelled him into the position as the leader of the radicals in the congress. This powerful group of legislators enacted harsh laws of retribution against the South after Lincoln's assassination and that period of post Civil War history called Radical Reconstructionism would become a dark page of American history whose deep scars would last for generations.

During the evening, the 5th New York Artillery band serenaded the President from the large public square fronting the Wills house. Inside the President and numerous guests attended the dinner party. Outside, loud voices from the crowd began calling for the President who then made an appearance at the door declaring, "In my position it is somewhat important that I should not say any foolish things (a rude voice shouted- If you can help it!) It very often happens that the only way to help it is to say nothing at all."[18] From here the crowd moved on to the homes where other celebrities were housed in an attempt to persuade them to speak. One blunt speech was given by Colonel John Forney, of Forney's War Press. Forney was also the secretary of the Senate.

He came out to the street crowd saying, "If I speak, I will speak my mind." Offended, that the President had not been received well, he exclaimed, "My friends, these are the first hearty cheers I have heard tonight. You gave no such cheers to your President down the street. Do you know what you owe that great man? You owe your country—you owe your name as American citizens." Continuing his criticism of the crowd for its apathy he then returned to eulogizing the President saying, "that great, wonderful, mysterious, inexplicable man, who holds in his single hands the reigns of the republic; who keeps his own counsels; who does his own purpose in his own way no matter what temporizing minister in his Cabinet sets himself up in opposition to the progress of the Age.[19]

Forney's astonishing candidness is explained by young John Hay, Lincoln's assistant secretary, who wrote in his diary about the various pranks and drinking parties going on about the town. Confessing to "a little whiskey" drinking, Hay wrote that Forney, "had been drinking a good deal during the day and was getting . . . ugly and dangerous."[20]

After witnessing Forney's exhortation, as well as the speech of the Secretary of State, William Seward, the crowd moved on. Wayne Mac Veagh, Chairman of the Republican Central Committee, who had witnessed the speeches went to a reception at the Wills house. Here, he recalled, "Lincoln . . . greatly enjoyed my account of the speeches of Mr. Seward and Colonel Forney. Soon afterward he said to me that he was about to withdraw because he wished to consider further the few words he was expected to say the next day."[21]

David Wills' house on Gettysburg Square—In this house President Lincoln spent the evening of November 18th and finished the composition of the Gettysburg Address. (NPS)

Lincoln's retirement to his room with canopied bed and small writing table was at 9:00 P.M. and was the time when he would complete the second page of The Gettysburg Address. His host, Mr. Wills, recorded this memory of the event:

> "After spending part of the evening in the parlor he retired to his room. He had his colored servant, William, with him. Between nine and ten o'clock the President sent his servant to request me to come to his room. I went and found him with paper prepared to write, and he said that he had just seated himself to put upon paper a few thoughts for the tomorrow's exercise, and had sent for me to ascertain what part he was to take in them. After a full talk I left him. About eleven o'clock he sent for me again, and when I went to his room he had the same paper in his hand, and asked me if he could see Mr. Seward. I told him Mr. Seward was staying with my neighbor, next door, and I would go and bring him over. He said "No, I'll go and see him." He went and I went with him and Mr. Lincoln carried the paper on which he had written his speech with him, and we found Mr. Seward and I left the President with him. In less than half an hour Mr. Lincoln returned with the paper in his hand."[22]

Lincoln's visit to his Secretary of State highlights the close relationship between the two men. Although there were great contrasts between the two, there were interesting similarities too. Both were born in the first decade of the century, both became attorneys, they once were both members of the Whig political party and both were early in their political careers opponents of slavery. That same year, 1858, that Lincoln became famous for his statement, "A house divided against itself cannot stand," Seward went into history with a similar prophetic and famous term that he called the "irrepressible conflict." Although rivals for the Republican Presidential nomination in 1860, Seward, a white haired sixty-year old former Senator from Auburn, New York, was now Lincoln's closest advisor and was previously responsible for substantial changes and additions to the President's First Inaugural Address as well as the decision to postpone the announcement of the Emancipation

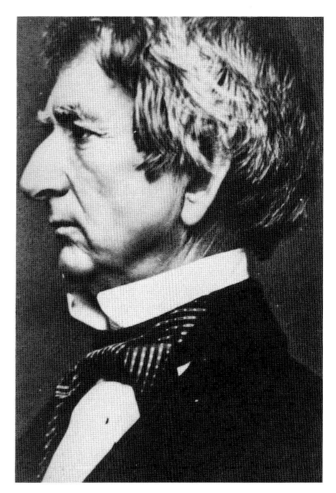

William Seward—Lincoln's closest advisor and the only known person Lincoln consulted on the writing of the Gettysburg Address. In 1867 he was scorned and maligned for being responsible for the "wasteful" expenditure of $7.2 million to acquire 586,412 square miles of territory that eventually became the nation's largest state, Alaska.

13

Ward Hill Lamon—This ex-brawler and banjo player was Lincoln's close personal friend, bodyguard and former law partner. A former Virginian, he was the Chief Marshal of the Gettysburg parade and cemetery ceremonies and the man who introduced the President to the audience at the historic moment of the Gettysburg Address. If Lincoln had not sent Lamon on a special mission in April of 1865, his presence and constant vigilance of the President's safety would have probably prevented the assassin John Wilkes Booth from murdering the President.

The President's Secretaries—A few days before the journey to Gettysburg President Lincoln sat for this photograph with his two personal secretaries, John G. Nicolay and John Hay (standing). Hay's diary contains intimate accounts of the various pranks, parties and carousing that went on in Gettysburg the night before the Cemetery dedication. Hay and Nicolay later collaborated on a massive ten volume history of Lincoln and Hay later became the U.S. Secretary of State under Presidents William Mckinley and Theodore Roosevelt.

Proclamation until a Union victory could be secured to enhance its political impact. His esteem for the President is reflected in this statement: ''Mr. Lincoln is the best man I ever knew.'' Both men would also suffer at the hands of assassins on the same day and as victims of the same conspiracy. On April 14, 1865, as the infamous assassin John Wilkes Booth was executing his foul plot to murder President Lincoln, Mr. Seward recovering from severe injuries sustained in a carriage accident was laid upon in his bedroom and sustained further severe injuries when stabbed in his bed by Booth's co-conspirator, Lewis Paine, who was once a soldier in the Confederate army until his capture at The Battle of Gettysburg.

Seward is not known to have had any influence upon the content of The Gettysburg Address but was certainly used as a sounding board to confirm the President's judgment regarding the content of the speech and whose expected delivery was now only hours away.

With the Lincoln-Seward conference concluded, the President departed the home of Seward's host, Robert Harper, and came out again upon York Street where the cheering throngs were waiting for him and where he announced, ''I can't speak tonight, gentlemen'' and then whispered to his bodyguard, Sergeant H. P. Bigham, ''You clear a way and I will hang on to your coat,'' whereupon he strode off at a rapid pace amidst tremendous cheering.

Lincoln then returned to his room for more work on the address and at a time that coincided with the late arrival of Governor Curtain and his party who had endured the aforementioned train breakdowns. Upon the governor's arrival at the Wills home he discovered—to his great dismay—that Mr. Wills had either invited too many guests for the available beds or had despaired of Curtain's arrival and had surrendered his bed to another in need. The final farce, played itself out on the eve of the impending solemn event at the cemetery and was recorded by the stately Everett himself. Registering his supreme disgust at the events that took place in the Wills home he wrote, "at first it was proposed to put the Governor into my bed with me. He kindly went and found lodging elsewhere . . . I did not get to bed till half past eleven; and the fear of having the Executive of Pennsylvania tumbled in upon me kept me awake till one."[24] And it didn't end there either! The liberal dispensation of numerous lodging invitations meant that Everett's elegant daughter Charlotte, was required to "bunk-up" with two other ladies in a single bed and the disgusting outcome was recorded when Everett noted that, "the bed broke down, and she betook herself to the floor."

At midnight the President received a welcome telegram from Mrs. Lincoln reporting that their son, Tad, who was ill was finally improving. Relieved by the news and needing to share it with someone Lincoln surprised Sergeant Bigham by suddenly opening his bedroom door, stepped into the hallway and said to the sentry, "That telegram was from home. My little boy is very sick, but is better." With this family footnote, the long day that had begun early in Washington had now ended late in Gettysburg.

For others in Gettysburg in search of lodging it was a bad situation that reporter John Russell Young described saying, "Gettysburg was in chaos over the new invasion and a corner in a tavern was a crowning mercy." A reporter for the Baltimore American described his plight that cold November night when he wrote, "After much fruitless inquiry some of our party were informed that several of the churches had considerably been thrown open by the citizens of Gettysburg to afford shelter to those who could not get lodging elsewhere, and to one of these about midnight, we were directed by a courteous soldier, and found already assembled quite a good congregation of sleepers, whose loud breathings and nasal accompaniments made a most inharmonious lullaby."

Day of Dedication

Promptly at 7:00 A.M., above the town on Cemetery Hill the battery commander barked his order and the gunners ignited their black gunpowder charges. Across the town citizens were awakened again, as they had been four months before, by the remembered sound of war: Boom! Ba-ba-boom-boom-boom! Ker-boom! Ker-boom-boom-boom! And again, they could feel the fear and know the unknowable as the artillery, instruments of death were now employed as a rude but powerful musical instrument to proclaim that the solemn moment of requiem had arrived.

Flags, black banners and black mourning bands were worn by many including the President who wore one around his tall black silk hat. He appeared at 10:00 a.m. at the York Street entrance to the Wills house where he provided the crowd its only amusing incident of the day. As the President mounted the horse assigned to him, he immediately smiled and the crowd laughed. It seems that the parade committee was unaware of Lincoln's six foot four inch stature and now, upon a small horse, his long legs nearly touched the ground. The parade was led off by the U.S. Marine Band and symbolically honored all three branches of service that had units in the battle by including each in the solemn procession. These were, of course, the infantry, artillery and cavalry.

The Solemn Procession—Looking north on Baltimore Street towards the center of Gettysburg is the solemn procession of civic, governmental and military figures as they turn right (your left) on their journey to Cemetery Hill. President Lincoln may be one of the tiny figures on horseback in the distance. (LC)

Following the President were the members of his cabinet, Edward Everett in a carriage, military bands playing their solemn dirges, a contingent of wounded from the battle—all accompanied by the rapid discharge of artillery. It was a powerful requiem for the dead. And amidst all, one would recall, "Then came the President easily distinguished from all others. He seemed the chief mourner."

In only a quarter of an hour the parade had journeyed south the three-quarter mile route to Cemetery Hill. There, seated upon a twenty foot platform of invited guests that included nine governors, three cabinet members, foreign diplomats, religious ministers and other civilian guests. The 12 × 20 foot wood platform had thirty chairs in three rows with the President seated in the middle of the front row, Mr. Everett to his right and Mr. Seward to his left. What a contrast! Flanked on one side by a cultured and classical scholar and orator on one side and on the other by a lover of the classics and Governor of New York by the age of thirty-three. The President in contrast was born in a log cabin in the Kentucky backwoods, his parents were both Virginians whose ancestry went back to England where the family emigrated to Massachusetts in 1638. Then, following the prevailing drift of American settlement they moved onward to New Jersey, Pennsylvania, and finally Virginia and Kentucky.

Lincoln was largely self taught and his experience included that of being a flatboat worker, attorney, member of the Illinois legislature, U.S. House of Representatives and now at the peak of a remarkable political career, President of the United States.

The Everett Oration

As planned, the consecration program began with a dirge by Birgfeld's Band of Philadelphia followed by a solemn prayer by Reverend T.H. Stockton, Chaplain of the United States Senate. The local newspaper reported that, after the prayer, "The most profound silence prevailed and many were affected by tears." But John Hay irreverently wrote in his diary, "Mr. Stockton made a prayer which thought it was an oration."[26]

Finally, it was Everett's turn, it was noon as he stood before the massed crowd of fifteen thousand atop Cemetery Hill. The reporter John Russell Young, remembered Everett's appearance and delivery, his "antique courtly ways, fine keen eyes, the voice of singular charm . . . the soft white hair, sunny, silken, clinging."[27]

Then, in the mild autumn temperature of 52 degrees, he began a learned and volumous two hour oration. It was the crowning pinnacle of his career and in its barest form would be like the traditional funeral orations since ancient times, a praise for the fallen and advice for the living. It began:

Standing beneath this serene sky, overlooking these broad fields now reposing from the labors of the waning year, the mighty Alleghenies dimly towering before us, the graves of our brethren beneath our feet, it is with hesitation that I raise my poor voice to break the eloquent silence of God and nature. But the duty to which you have called me must be performed; grant me, I pray you, your indulgence and your sympathy.

The first sentence of the oration consisted of 52 words; another would run 106 words.

The address was filled with classical and historical allusions. But everything would relate to the Cemetery's consecration. Some passages would even be strikingly similar to those of Lincoln. Everett said, for example, "We have assembled . . . to pay the last tribute of respect to the brave men who . . . nobly sacrificed their lives that their fellow men may live." His resonant and strong voice refuted the pretense that, "the war is one of self-defense, waged for the right of self-government." He compared Union General Meade, the victor at Gettysburg, to the Duke of Wellington and the battle to that of Waterloo. A detailed narrative of the battle with troop movements as well as the role of the senior commanders was also presented.

Then he paid honor to the brethern and sisters of Christian benevolence who hastened to the battlefield, "to moisten the parched tongue, to bind the ghastly wounds, to soothe the parting agonies alike of friend and foe, and to catch the last whispered message of love from dying lips." He particularly paid tribute to the women who, "in the hospital and the tents . . . have rendered services which millions could not buy."

Then he posed the question, "Which of the two parties to the war is responsible for all this suffering?" Answering his own question, he said that it was Jefferson Davis and aspiring politicians, "in danger of losing their monopoly of its offices" in government. Then, thundering in waves of verbal emotion fired out to the crowd, he proclaimed that the rebellion was a crime and treason by "the degenerate sons of America . . . hard-hearted men whose cruel lust of power has brought this desolating war upon the land." And to hide "the deformity of the crime," he argued, the successionists claimed that the "States are 'Sovereigns'." He derided this argument saying that the Constitution, "nowhere recognizes the states as 'Sovereigns,' in fact, that, by their names it does not recognize them at all; while the authority established by that instrument is recognized . . . as 'the Government of the United States'." Furthermore he added, to yield to southern demands and acknowledge Confederate independence would result in two hostile governments "with a certainty of further disintegration and result in hideous national suicide."

Countering the argument of some in both the North and South that it was too late for a harmonious restoration of the Union he reviewed the wars and rebellions of Europe and how they had eventually led to national brotherhood. He argued that, "The bonds that unite us as one people . . . of origin, language, belief, and law . . . are of perennial force and energy."

Finally, in the concluding moments of the oration, he proclaimed:

> God bless the Union, it is dearer to us for the blood of brave men which has been shed in its defense . . . All time is the millenium of their glory . . . as we bid farewell to the dust of these martyr-heroes, that wheresoever throughout the civilized world the accounts of this great warfare are read, and down to the latest period of recorded time, in the glorious annals of our common country, there will be no brighter page than that which relates the Battle of Gettysburg.[28]

Loud applause now swept through the crowd as the President stood to shake the hand of Everett saying, "I am grateful to you."[29] Then, following a dirge by the Baltimore Glee Club, the Chief Marshall of the ceremonies, presidential bodyguard and ex-Virginian, Ward Lamon, stepped forward to announce, "The President of the United States."

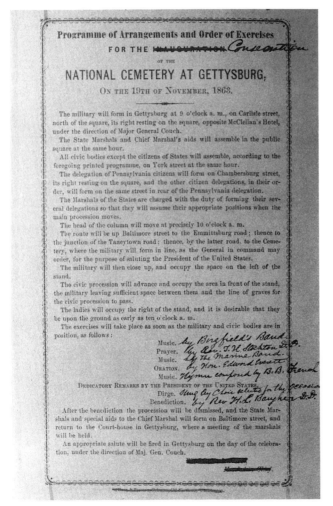

Dedication Day Program—Facets of Edward Everett's personality can be discerned from his copy of the Dedication Program. The program was printed in Washington by Ward Hill Lamon, Chief Marshal of the District of Columbia. Angered that the program listed the President but not Everett, the main orator of the day, Everett crossed out Lamon's name at the bottom of the program, his title of Marshal in Chief (of the procession) and even that of the Washington printer listed at the very bottom of the program. Note also the word crossed out at the top. Everett could not resist crossing out the word "inauguration", incorrectly used, and writing in the more correct word, "consecration".

The Gettysburg Address

It was two-o'clock as Lincoln's tall thin figure stepped to the front of the wooden platform. Those close enough could see that his black suit matched his dark hair and small gray eyes and that his tall stature complimented his high forehead and cheekbones. As the applause died away, his strong but sad face became animated as he began those cadenced passages that would combine Jefferson's ideals of freedom and equality with the Christian concept of life, death and rebirth becoming a part of the battle itself and giving a symbolic significance to the military events that it had lacked:

> Fourscore and seven years ago our fathers brought forth on this continent a new nation, conceived in liberty, and dedicated to the proposition that all men are created equal.
> Now we are engaged in a great Civil War, testing whether that nation, or any nation so conceived and so dedicated can long endure. We are met on a great battlefield of that war.
> We have come to dedicate a portion of that field as a final resting place for those who here gave their lives that nation might live. It is altogether fitting and proper that we should do this. But in a larger sense we cannot dedicate we cannot consecrate, we cannot hallow this ground. The brave men, living and dead, who struggled here, have conscrated it far above our poor power to add or detract. The world will little note, nor long remember, what we say here, but it can never forget what they did here. It is for us, the living, rather to be dedicated here to the unfinished work which they who fought here have thus far so nobly advanced. It is rather for us to be here dedicated to the great task remaining before us, that from these honored dead we take increased devotion to that cause for which they gave the last full measure of devotion: that we here highly resolve that these dead shall not have died in vain: that this nation, under God, shall have a new birth of freedom, and that this government of the people, by the people, and for the people shall not perish from the earth.

In a short two minutes it was over. The stunned crowd, surprised by the brevity, paused to ask themselves if it was really over. Then, applause broke out. The unseated crowd had been on its feet for four hours.

It is said that there is genius in brevity. Nowhere is this better exemplified than in Lincoln's shortest but most famous address. Tradition says that the Lincoln brevity began in his youthful backwoods days when he was forced to learn writing skills with a piece of charcoal upon the limited space of a farm shovel. In any event, his enduring stature as America's most revered president is in part attributable to his ability to express sublime thoughts in simple language.

The Address, later revised by Lincoln himself, would contain 271 words in ten sentences and no word was over four syllables long. But in that Address there was created the most beautiful and politically significant document in the English speaking world. The sentences, outwardly smooth, were inside filled with the enigmas of the unique American experiment.

Close up view of the Speaker's Platform November 19th, 1863—The photograph was taken as Edward Everett (right arrow) was being escorted to his seat beside the President, before the dedication program began. President Lincoln is seated left center with bowed head possibly reading either his address or the program. Sec. of State William Seward is seated to Lincoln's left seen in the photograph in profile. The beaded man with the top hat is Ward Hill Lamon, while the man seated to Lincoln's right is John Nicolay one of Lincoln's personal secretaries. (National Archives)

The central theme was one he had raised before when he wrote, "Is there in all republics this inherent and fatal weakening? Must a government, of necessity, be too strong for the liberties of its own people, or too weak to maintain its own existence?" This was not a rhetorical question. Certainly not in the great trial of the Republic in 1863 nor was it in the minds of the Founding Fathers less than a century before when one of them, John Adams, stated, "Remember, democracy never lasts long. It soon wastes, exhausts and murders itself. There never was a democracy that did not commit suicide." Lincoln, however, believed that out of the turmoil, out of the mystical cords of memory, there could emerge a new birth of freedom, a new nation made stronger by the proposition that all men were created equal.

That night as his train rumbled into the darkness, no one could have realized that that day, Pennsylvania, site of The Declaration of Independence, then The Constitution of the United States had now become the birthplace of the nation's third greatest document, The Gettysburg Address.

How the Gettysburg Address Transformed America

Caught up in the eloquence of the Gettysburg Address, we, as a nation, have been negligent regarding its more meaningful aspect: How the Address transformed the nation by changing and perfecting the Constitution.

To grasp the enormity of it all we must understand that in 1863 the United States was the largest slaveholding nation in the world and in spite of the fact that the Declaration of Independence declared that "All men are created equal"—a fact disputed by Senator John Pettit of Indiana who called that principal not "a self-evident truth" but instead "a self-evident lie."[29] Although Lincoln called Pettit's statement "shameful," he would have had to agree with the senator that the U.S. Constitution said nothing of equality of men and in fact guaranteed inequality by Article IV, Section 3, of the document whereby the creators of the Constitution, ashamed before the world to state specifically what they were adopting, proclaimed that, "No person held under service or labor . . . shall in consequence . . . be discharged from such service or labor . . . to whom such service or labor may be due.'' That legacy, the worst given to us by Great Britain would haunt the nation from its infancy and be a malignant heritage recognized by essayist John Jay Chapman when he wrote, ''There was never a moment during the earliest days of our national history when the slavery issue was not a sleeping serpent. That issue lay coiled up under the table during the deliberations of the Constitutional Convention in 1787.'' Lincoln, and all of those knowledgeable about the Constitution recognized that it represented a gross contradiction from the original ideals of human equality that the revolutionary fervor of the moment had wrought in the Declaration of Independence. Lincoln clearly understood that because of the enormous economic interests related to slavery, the Founding Fathers could not confront nor compromise on it. Instead, he strongly believed that the Fathers of the Constitution, to their everlasting credit, recognized the inherent evil of slavery, expected that it would die of its own destructive malignancy and confirmed that judgement by prohibiting slavery's expansion and leaving the fullness of time to allow the Constitution to flower into the perfected instrument promised by the Declaration of Independence. The ''sleeping serpent'' however was awakened and let loose in 1854 with the passage of the Kansas-Nebraska Act that repealed the restriction on slavery's expansion and made it a legitimate and permanent ''institution.'' Lincoln believed that this Act profaned the sentiments of the Declaration and violated the Constitution. Even worse, he believed a conspiracy had been hatched to make slavery legal in every state and territory of the Union and recorded his moral and political outrage after the Act's passage by stating, ''Our republican robe is soiled, and trailed in the dust'' but in a prophetic comment that followed added, ''Let us repurify it.''

No other political event in Lincoln's life had the impact upon him as the passage of the Act. It lit a burning fire within him that in turn galvanized him as no other event ever did. It was the watershed political event of his life and propelled him back into a political career that had previously gone nowhere. Ironically, the attempt to expand slavery was the cause of its ultimate extinction as Lincoln riding the tide of history used the chaos and upheaval of Civil War to launch a second political revolution by transforming the Constitution that in turn transformed a nation.

It was not launched without protest, however, by those astute observers who saw the ominous portent of what that revolution could represent. If, for example, the Constitution became a ''living'' document meant to change with the times (and as we know it to be today) could it not then be degraded and debased to mean anything or everything dependent upon the particular passion of the moment? Or, to put it another way, if it were allowed to be changed in a manner unrestrained and absolute, could it not then become absolutely unrestrained? Taking note of, and correctly judging the revolutionary aspects of the Gettysburg Address,

The Chicago Sun-Times registered its outrage at what it regarded as a betrayal of the Constitution and Lincoln's oath of office when it wrote: ''Mr Lincoln did most foully traduce the motives of the men who were slain at Gettysburg,'' when he referred to ''a new birth of freedom,'' explaining that ''They gave their lives to maintain the old government and the only Constitution and Union.'' It was a perversion of history and an ''ignorant rudeness'' that insulted the dead. Then, with no quarter given to the embattled President from the newspaper's own homestate, they continued to pile it on when they asserted that, ''Readers will not have failed to observe the exceeding bad taste which characterized the remarks of the President and Secretary of State at the dedication of the Soldiers' cemetery at Gettysburg. The cheek of every American must tingle with shame as he reads the silly, flat, and dish-watery utterances of the man who has to be pointed out to intelligent foreigners as the President of the United States.''[30]

In the end, Lincoln's vision of that perfected instrument, that new Constitution, that new nation he proposed in his address at Gettysburg would become a reality as the original Articles of it would soon be re-interpreted and new ones added by judges and legislators sympathetic to the struggle and memory of a martyred president. How the nation was forever transformed can be seen in the changes to the Constitution. Where the first eleven of twelve amendments limited the powers of the national government six of the next seven expanded them and reduced those of the individuals and the states. None can argue against those perfecting Amendments enacting that postponed promise of equality. Lost though in the transformation was that other precious gift of the revolution: That revolutionary principle that the government that governed least was best and that constitutionally guaranteed rights of the individual would be unassailable and not reduced. No one can dispute this fact: What the Constitution represented before Lincoln was not what it would come to be after him. For the people and the courts of the North it became a peaceful political revolution. For the South it would be imposed by the force of arms.

The Lost Cemetery Photographs

Until 1952 no one knew that any photograph had been taken of the Gettysburg Cemetery dedication. That was the year however that Josephine Cobb, a specialist in photography at the National Archives came across a negative filed under the heading ''Crowd of Citizens, Soldiers etc.''

Curious as to the image of the large crowd and enlarging it she became intrigued by the discovery of several prominent figures that she was able to discern. By the process of elimination she was able to determine that the people on the photograph were together at only one possible public ceremony—The dedication of the Gettysburg National Cemetery on November 19, 1863.

The image and several other photographs of the event

were discovered among the collection of Mathew Brady and presumed to have been taken by his firm. Brady most likely had purchased the photographs for his own collection and inventoried them as his own pictures as was his custom with all of the photographs purchased or taken by his own employees. With poor eyesight Brady acted as a supervisor to those employees and perhaps took no Civil War pictures himself.*

Nearly a decade after her discovery of the Gettysburg photograph Miss Cobb uncovered a letter misplaced in the records of the U.S. Patent Office that documents the true identity of the photographers at the cemetery event. Surprisingly, they turned out to be the Weaver family, one of whom, Samuel, was also the Superintendent of Exhumation of the Gettysburg battle dead and a member of a family of photographers (Samuel of Gettysburg, Peter of nearby Hanover and William of Baltimore.)

The letter, written less than a week after the dedication, not only confirms the identity of the photographers but also displays the poor education of its author and explains the numerous errors of spelling upon the tombstones of the soldiers in the cemetery. Weaver was Gettysburg's first resident photographer and opened a gallery in the town in 1852. (Please note that the letter, written by Samuel to his brother William was written by an uneducated man and contains numerous mis-spellings, incorrect punctuation, etc. It and all of the subsequent soldiers' letters quoted later in this study are left unedited to preserve their historical accuracy.)

> Brother I wish you could have been here on the 19th last at the dedication of the National Cemetery it was one of the largest assembling that ever met in our country with the exception when the battle was fought, it is supposed that there were not less than from 30 to 40,000 strangers present, & the order of the day was so excelent everthing was done in peace & harmony, I dident see one drunken man all day nor evening, though I was kept very buisey all day, in the fore noon I assisted Peter of getting a negative of the large assembly on the cemetery ground which I think is very fine, we have not as yet printed any shot of the negative Peter went off to Hanover on last Sunday evening to attend to his car again, I suppose he has printed some shots of the assembly that was at the dedication of the 19th, I have had Peter at G. for 7 weeks taking negatives of the surgeons the hospital tents at the General Hospitals, he has some very fine negatives, we have sold over 1000 shots up to this time, we have something like 75 different negatives, I intend as soon as all the dead soldiers are burried in the National Cemetery, to take a picture of the whole ground & also take a negative of the ground for each state, Brother it is going to make one of the pertiest cemetary in U.S. I have been employed by the government to superintend the raising of all the dead that fell on the battle fields at G. & all that died in the hospitals to the N. Cemetery in 20 days I sent 1285, If the weather remains favourable I think that I can have them all sent in by the first of Jan. Please let me hear from you soon, Yours in love & cc.[31]
>
> S. Weaver

Peter Weaver—This Gettysburg area photographer, lost in photographic history for over a century, took the photographs of Lincoln and the dedication of the Gettysburg National Cemetery. His decision to do so may have been influenced by Samuel Weaver who was in charge of the Gettysburg burials. (Courtesy of Gregory Coco and the Nicholas G. Wilson Memorial Library and Research Center, Aspers, Pa.)

Lincoln and the Long Road to the Gettysburg Address

Who was this man who came out of the West like a giant shooting star illuminating the night and suddenly disappearing again?

Born in a log cabin in Kentucky on February 12, 1809 Lincoln would grow up to greatness on the American frontier of Indiana and Illinois despite poverty and the unrelenting harshness of the untamed wilderness. When only ten years old Abraham was kicked by a horse rendering him unconscious and afflicting him with a morbid melancholy that became his unwelcome companion the rest of his life. The harshness of the frontier was also matched by the harshness of an unloving, rude and irresponsible father. Once, in the presence of others, Tom Lincoln struck Abraham such a violent blow to the face that it knocked him to the ground.

* During the November 19th Gettysburg ceremony Brady was at his New York City studio supervising the taking of the photographic portraits of the Russian Naval Officers of the czarist's fleet who were visiting the port until November 23rd. This visit of the Russian Fleet was one of the great diplomatic sensations of the Civil War.

That unhappy childhood was a bitter memory that the sensitive and vulnerable child never forgave nor forgot. Just before his father's death in 1851 Lincoln wrote, "Say to him that if we could meet now it is doubtful whether it would not be more painful than pleasant."[32]

Lincoln had only a year of formal schooling and admitted once that he did not study grammar until the age of 23. He had a thirst for learning though and once walked eighteen miles to borrow a book. He once said that, as a boy, he had gone to school "by littles—a little now and a little then."

How then did this child of poverty ride the waves of history from dimly lit log cabins to crystalled chandeliered halls? And how did it happen that he would also become a lord of language creating such letters and speeches of such striking simplicity and eloquence as to set him apart in classic greatness? It was a greatness of character, superior intellect and most of all a driving ambition to succeed.

His effective technique as a writer can be traced to the Bible and he would frequently use its literary style and content. He could astonish visitors with his knowledge of certain passages in the Bible and his biblical allusions in his papers and speeches can be traced to twenty-two different books of the Old and New Testaments. William Shakespeare was another influence and his interest in and study of all forms of communication can be seen in his own creations of poetry. As a speaker, he had a natural ability to mimic others. His neighbors could recall to their amusement how Lincoln loved to climb on a fence and, like an actor, mimic the grandiose style of the visiting frontier preachers. His powers of observation of others and their techniques followed by his own testing and experiences of those techniques all provided a fertile testing ground that eventually allowed him to develop the ability to effectively use words as a perfected instrument to convince juries and then, later in life, to speak to and lead an entire nation.

Lincoln also had a strong moral fervor that was tempered towards moderation and conciliation as well as a personal temperament marked by kindliness and sympathy that gave him a spiritual quality rare in a successful politician. It was once said of him that he loved his enemies more than he loved himself. Writing to his friend, Joshua Speed, he once said, "You know well that I do not feel my own sorrows much more keenly than I do yours."

At the age of 21 the Lincolns migrated to Illinois where Abraham became a rail splitter and flatboatman, and then settled in New Salem as a storekeeper, postmaster and surveyor. He enlisted as a volunteer in the Black Hawk Indian War and after that considered blacksmithing as an occupation but finally decided to study law. Then he moved on to the new state capitol of Springfield, kept busy by traveling the court circuit and became one of the most distinguished and successful Illinois attorneys. His political career in state and national politics reflected a recurring theme that he found both intriguing and challenging: The promise and problems of self-government.

Lincoln's political career in Illinois came into national prominence in 1858 during his U.S. senatorial debate with Stephen Douglas when he said,

"A house divided against itself cannot stand. I believe this government cannot endure permanently half slave and half free. I do not expect the Union to be dissolved—I do not expect the house to fall—but I do expect it will cease to be divided. It will become all one thing, or all the other."[33]

The words, as though from a prophet, accurately predicted the course of the Union in the years that would follow. That cause of the divided house, slavery, was an evil that he had expressed his feelings about in other addresses when he explained,

"I hate it because it deprives our republican example of its just influence in the world; enables the enemies of free institutions with plausibility to taunt us as hypocrites . . . When the white man governs himself, that is self-government; but when he governs himself and also governs another man, that is more than self-government—that is despotism . . . The deceitful cloak of 'self-government'; wherewith the sum of all villainies seeks to protect and adorn itself, must be torn from its hateful carcass . . . Those who deny freedom to others deserve it not for themselves, and, under a just God, cannot long retain it."[34]

As the conflict came and as Lincoln stepped on the national stage as the nation's sixteenth president he proclaimed:

"In your hands, my dissatisfied fellow-countrymen, and not in mine, is the momentous issue of civil war. The government will not assail you. You can have no conflict without being yourselves the aggressors. You have no oath registered in heaven to destroy the government, while I shall have the most solemn one to preserve, protect, and defend it."

"I am loath to close. We are not enemies, but friends. We must not be enemies. Though passion may have strained, it must not break our bonds of affection. The mystic chords of memory, stretching from every battlefield and patriot grave to every living heart and hearth-stone all over this broad land, will yet swell the chorus of the Union when again touched, as surely they will be, by the better angels of our nature."[35]

The Second Inaugural: Lincoln's Other Great Address

Besides the Gettysburg Address, Lincoln's other wartime masterpiece of modern English eloquence was the Second Inaugural Address of 1865. Noteworthy for its deep moral and religious tones, the address reveals Lincoln's belief in the divine retribution for the sins of slavery and the concept of the sins of the fathers being visited upon the children of another generation and "a truth," he later wrote "which I thought needed to be told." The address was his last as President before a large audience:

"The Almighty has his own purposes. 'Woe unto the world because of offenses! For it must needs be that offenses come; but woe to that man by whom the offense cometh'. If we shall suppose that American slavery is one of those offenses which, in the providence of God, must needs come, but which, having continued through His appointed time, He now wills to remove, and that He gives to both North and South this terrible war, as the woe due to those by whom the offense came, shall we discern therein any departure from those divine attributes which the believers in a living God always ascribe to Him? Fondly do we hope—fervently do we pray—that this mighty scourge of war may speedily pass away. Yet, if God wills that it continue until all the wealth piled by the bondsman's two hundred and fifty years of unrequited toil shall be sunk, and until every drop of blood drawn with the lash shall be paid by another drawn with the sword, as was said three thousand years ago, so still it must be said, ''The judgments of the Lord are true and righteous altogether.''

With malice toward none; with charity for all; with firmness in the right, as God gives us to see the right, let us strive on to finish the work we are in; to bind up the nation's wounds; to care for him who shall have borne the battle, and for his widow, and his orphan—to do all which may achieve and cherish a just and lasting peace among ourselves, and with all nations.''[36]

As the address was being delivered at the Capitol, the clouds which had been hiding the sun suddenly were parted to bathe the crowd as if in heavenly enlightenment, and, as if in recognition of some divine intervention upon what would be Lincoln's most deeply religious address, the crowd in turn responded with a resounding cheer.

Soon the President departed amidst the thundering salute of the artillery that reverberated across the city to announce to the world that the life of the Republic continued and endured.

In a few short weeks however, Lincoln would return to the Capitol and under its massive dome lie in state before the people he had served and after being murdered by the forces of hatred and injustice that he had sought to overcome. And, as one said, ''Now he belongs to the ages.''

A Guide Through the National Cemetery

President John F. Kennedy once said, ''A nation reveals itself not only by the men it produces but also by the men it honors, the men it remembers.'' As a nation Americans both remember and revere their national heritage as much or more than any other nation. True too is the fact that the sun never sets on the graves of American servicemen nor upon the Americans who regularly visit them.

Understanding our turbulent past makes us less impatient with the turbulent present. It also fosters patriotism and a sense of roots and values in an ever increasing rootless and valueless society. The peace and quiet of the Cemetery is a good place to pause and reflect upon our lives and our values. For the patriots of sixty-three it was a time worth living in and for us a time worth remembering and under-

The Lincoln Speech Memorial, erected in 1912.

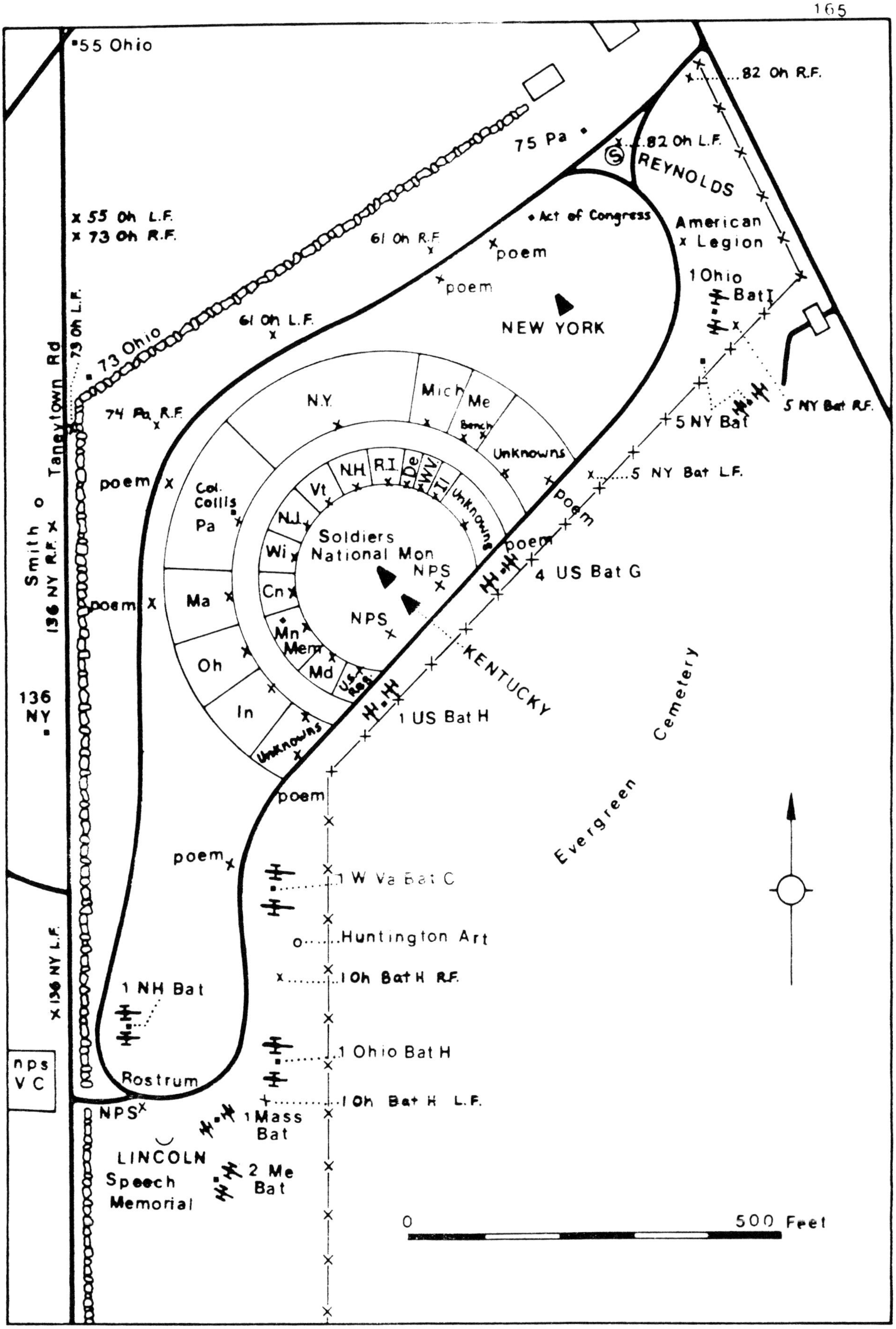

- 55 Ohio

x 82 Oh R.F.

75 Pa

..82 Oh L.F.

(S) REYNOLDS

x 55 Oh L.F.
x 73 Oh R.F.

61 Oh R.F.

- Act of Congress

poem

American
x Legion

73 Oh L.F.

73 Ohio

61 Oh L.F.

poem

NEW YORK

1 Ohio
Bat I

x

74 Pa R.F.

N.Y.

Mich Me

Bench

Unknowns

5 NY Bat R.F.

5 NY Bat

poem x

Col.
Collis
Pa

Vt

NH R.I. De WV Il

Unknown

x....5 NY Bat L.F.

Smith o Taneytown Rd

136 NY R.F. x

poem x

N.J.

Wi

Soldiers
National Mon
NPS

poem

poem

4 US Bat G

Ma

Cn

NPS

poem X

Mn
Mem

136
NY

Oh

Md

KENTUCKY

Evergreen Cemetery

In

Unknowns

1 US Bat H

poem

x 136 NY L.F.

poem

1 W Va Bat C

o......Huntington Art

x......1 Oh Bat H R.F.

1 NH Bat

1 Ohio Bat H

nps
V C

Rostrum

1 Oh Bat H L.F.

NPS X

1 Mass Bat

LINCOLN
Speech
Memorial

2 Me Bat

0   500 Feet

23

standing. Somehow though the complete grasp of the meaning of all of this and the personal emotional relevance to us is not possible without considering the flesh and blood history of those involved as individuals rather than collectively the overall events as a whole. This then, is the purpose of the second part of this history.

So we now invite you to join us for a personal walk of reverence and remembrance through the grounds of the Gettysburg National Cemetery, or, in lieu of that, a journey by way of the pictures and pages of this history that we now continue.

We recommend that you begin your walking tour through the National Cemetery at its western gate, across from the Visitor Center of the National Park Service. Please be advised that no food, drink, nor pets are allowed within the Cemetery grounds.

As you enter the Cemetery you will notice before you a large red brick rostrum. This rostrum was constructed in 1879 and is used for numerous memorial services throughout the year. Several American Presidents have either spoken or sat upon this platform during services (Rutherford B. Hayes, Theodore Roosevelt, Calvin Coolidge, Herbert Hoover, Franklin D. Roosevelt, and Dwight D. Eisenhower), as well as other notable individuals, more recently; General Colin Powell.

Opposite the rostrum is the impressive Lincoln Speech Memorial, erected in 1912 to commemorate President Lincoln's Gettysburg Address. This memorial however does not mark the site where Abraham Lincoln delivered his famous speech. We will walk to and discuss that site later during this tour. The bust of Lincoln on this monument is the work of the renowned sculptor Henry K. Bush-Brown and is considered a superb portrait of Lincoln, displaying upon his face the stress that the war had thrust upon him. Inscribed upon the right hand plaque of the memorial are the words Lincoln spoke that afternoon of November 19th, comprising the Gettysburg Address. On the left hand plaque is the personal letter of invitation that David Wills sent to the President which reads in part:

"... It is the desire that you as Chief Executive of the Nation formally set apart these grounds to their sacred use by a few appropriate remarks. It will be a source of great gratification to the many widows and orphans that have been made almost friendless by the great battle here to have you here personally and it will kindle anew in the breasts of the comrades of these brave dead who are now in the tented field or nobly meeting the foe in the front a confidence that they who sleep in death on the battlefield are not forgotten by those highest in authority and they will feel that should their fate be the same their remains will not be uncared for."

Attention should be drawn to Wills' statement that the committee wished the President to say, "a few appropriate remarks." The President was not to be the key-note speaker at the dedication of the Cemetery; that honor was to be given to the famous orator Mr. Edward Everett. Several days before Lincoln traveled to Gettysburg, in reply to the noted newsman Noah Brooks, he had said that his speech would be "short, short, short."

Behind the Lincoln Speech Memorial are row upon row of stones marking the resting places of veterans other than

The Speaker's Rostrum, built in 1879.

those of the Gettysburg battle. The Gettysburg National Cemetery is the oldest National Cemetery in the United States. Within these sacred grounds lie over 7,000 men and women who served our country in war and peace—from the Civil War through the Vietnam Conflict. Since 1972 the Cemetery has been closed for any new burial sites.

Continue your tour by walking along the upper driveway keeping the iron fence to your immediate right.

As you walk through the Cemetery you will surely notice the magnificent vegetation: Norway Maple, Silver Fur, Bald Cypress, Eastern Hemlock (State tree of Pennsylvania), Buckeye, Holly, European Purple Beech, Ginko and others. Most of the trees have small identifying plaques. During the battle this section of the Cemetery was a cornfield, thus these beautiful and ancient trees were not growing here. Many of the trees you see today were brought and planted within the Cemetery in the early 1870s, some being large even at that time. The individual who was responsible for the landscaping of the Cemetery was William Sanders, who is also known for the landscaping of other American cemeteries such as Mount Auburn in Cambridge, Massachusetts. There is however one tree you will pass which did stand upon this hill during the battle. It is a Honey Locust which is to the right of the upper drive close to the iron fence.

The iron fence, which separates the local Evergreen Cemetery from the National Cemetery, has a unique history in its own right. In 1863 it stood across from the White House in Washington enclosing part of Lafayette Square. In 1933 it was placed in its present location.

The Evergreen Cemetery was established by the town in 1853, just ten years before the two armies would struggle to possess these heights. There are many grave stones that pre-date 1853, but this is due to the fact that the churches of the town transferred the bodies from their graveyards to the Evergreen Cemetery after it was established. This cemetery has many individuals of local interest as well as national fame. Persons such as; James Gettys, the founder of the town, John Burns, who at almost the age of 70 fought during the first day's battle, David Wills, who invited President Lincoln to Gettysburg, poet Marianne Moor, Eddie Plank who pitched for the Philadelphia Athletics and who was inducted into the Baseball Hall of Fame, and Mary Virginia (Jennie) Wade, who was the only civilian killed during the battle.

There are several headstones visible from the fence which were damaged by artillery fire during the engagement. One such headstone is that of Sergeant Frederick Huber of the 23rd Pennsylvania Regiment. Sergeant Huber had been killed at the Battle of Fair Oaks, Virginia, May 31, 1862. His father had brought his son's body back home, interring him in the Evergreen Cemetery. At some time during the battle, possibly during the frightful artillery shelling of the 3rd day, Huber's headstone was struck and broken. It stands today, unrepaired, as a mute reminder that war is respectful of no one, not even the dead.

Sgt. Frederick Huber, 23rd Pa. Infantry, killed at Fair Oaks, Va. May 31, 1862. (23rd Pa. Regimental)

The broken headstone of Sgt. Frederick Huber in the Evergreen Cemetery.

The cannon and monuments that you are passing mark battle positions of different Union units: 2nd Maine Battery, 1st Massachusetts Light Battery, 1st Ohio Battery H and 1st West Virginia Battery C. It should be remembered that at the time of the battle this hill was a critical section of the Union defensive line. Most artillery pieces that mark the battlefield are Civil War period guns, but they were not necessarily used during the Gettysburg battle.

You will soon see on your left two plaques with a poem written upon them.

> The muffled drum's sad roll has beat
>   the soldier's last tattoo.
> No more on life's parade shall meet
>   that brave and fallen few.
>
> On fame's eternal camping ground,
>   their silent tents are spread,
> And glory guards with solemn round,
>   the bivouac of the dead.

This poem entitled, "The Bivouac of the Dead," was written by Theodore O'Hara to honor Americans slain in the Battle of Buena Vista (1847) during the Mexican War. Throughout the Cemetery you will see other stanzas of this solemn tribute.

As you continue along the drive, you will pass one end of the semicircular Union burial plots. The row upon row of single stones with numbers carved upon them compose one of three sections of unknown plots. Within the total semicircular burial site, there are over 1,600 unknown soldiers of the Gettysburg battle, but 979 of these are classified as totally unknown. When the dead were being transferred from their battlefield graves to the present Cemetery, great effort was used to identify the bodies, but needless to say, not all could be identified. However, the state and even some of the regiments these unknowns served in could be identified because of the uniform buttons, belt buckles, etc. that were worn. These men would be buried as unknown in their respective state plots. But for 979 men, even the state they served from could not be verified, thus they were buried with these individually numbers stones as totally unknown. Discussion of the three unknown plots will be taken up later when we visit specific graves within the semicircle, since a few of these unknowns have now been identified through research.

Continue to walk along the driveway, stopping at the monument of the 1st United States Artillery, Battery H.

The two cannon on either side of the monument are 12 pounder bronze smoothbores, commonly referred to as "Napoleons." The cannon on the right as you look at the monument, has inscribed on its muzzle the name of the foundry, "Revere Copper Co." This is the same Revere who in 1775 rode from Boston to warn the countryside that "the British were coming." He was a coppersmith and after the American Revolution founded the firm that manufactured many of the Union Napoleons used during the Civil War. Another interesting feature of this artillery piece is the dent on its side, caused by the impact of an enemy projec-

tile. Also note, that this barrel has been placed on the reproduction carriage up-side down.

A few more steps will bring you to a tall imposing memorial which sits at the center of the semicircular burial plots.

This is the Soldiers' National Monument completed in the year of 1869, making it the second oldest memorial on the Gettysburg battlefield. Around its base are four Carrara marble figures, carved by the famous sculptor Randolph

Dented artillery barrel of the 1st U.S. Artillery Battery H.

Rogers. The woman holding a sheaf of wheat represents Ceres the goddess of "Plenty," while the woman holding the book and pen, Clio by name, symbolizes "History." The statues of the two men symbolize "War," represented by a Union soldier, and "Peace," which is portrayed uniquely by a mechanic holding a hammer and a large cog resting beside him. Special attention should be taken to the chairs each figure is sitting upon, as they are filled with classical symbolism. The memorial is surmounted by a statue entitled "The Genius of Liberty." She clutches in her left hand a sword of war, while holding in her right hand the laurel wreath of victory.

At the foot of the Soldiers' National Monument rests a smaller memorial erected in 1975 by the State of Kentucky. This memorial is in honor of Kentucky's native son, Abraham Lincoln and the speech which he delivered on November 19th, near this spot. Lincoln's immortal Address in his handwriting is reproduced in bronze upon this unassuming monument.

There are five authenticated drafts of the Gettysburg Address presently known and preserved. Lincoln's first draft, the "Nicolay Copy," consists of two sheets of paper. The first sheet was written shortly before Lincoln traveled to

The Soldiers' National Monument, second oldest monument upon the Gettysburg battlefield, dedicated in 1869.

The Soldiers' National Monument under construction in 1869. (NPS)

Gettysburg. It is written in ink on Executive Mansion stationary, not on an envelope as legend says. Once in Gettysburg, Lincoln finished the speech using paper given to him by David Wills, in whose house Lincoln spent the evening. This second page is written in pencil. It is widely accepted that these two sheets of paper were held by Lincoln when he delivered his speech.

Afterwards, Lincoln would rewrite his speech several times at the requests of persons who desired copies, and each time changes would appear. We know that even as he delivered the speech, he did not follow his written text verbatim, but added words and phrases such as "under God." Thus all five copies which President Lincoln wrote are slightly different from each other.

The first (Nicolay Copy) and second (Hay Copy) drafts are owned by the Library of Congress in Washington, D.C. The third draft (Everett Copy) is in the State Historical Library, Springfield, Illinois. The fourth (Bancroft Copy) is owned by Cornell University, Ithaca, New York, while the final draft (Bliss Copy) which is considered the standard version, resides today in the Lincoln Room of the White House.

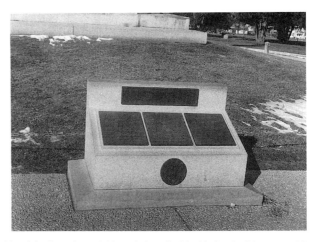

Lincoln's Gettysburg Address is inscribed in his handwriting upon this memorial erected in 1976 by the State of Kentucky.

War

History

Liberty, surmounting the column of the
Soldiers' National Monument.

Peace

Plenty

The Site Where the Gettysburg Address was Delivered

Since 1863, several locations as to where the dedication platform stood and thus where the greatest speech in American history was delivered, have been proposed and argued. One of the first was the Selleck site, "located 40 feet northeast of the outer circle of soldiers' graves" beyond the New York State plot. The premise for this site comes from Mr. W. Yates Selleck, who was the Wisconsin commissioner on the Soldiers' Cemetery board, and who was seated on the platform that 19th of November. In Selleck's personal copy of the Report of the Select Committee of the Soldiers' National Cemetery published in 1865, he drew a rectangle on the map of the cemetery, thus supposedly marking the site of the platform. Since Mr. Selleck sat on the platform, his location of where that platform stood should be creditable.

The second and traditional platform site is where the Soldiers' National Monument is presently located, within the semicircular burial plots.

National Park Service historians and the authors of this book have concluded that both of these sites are erroneous. It is now accepted through photographic evidence, that the platform stood a few yards east of the Soldiers' National Monument, just beyond the iron fence within the Evergreen Cemetery. Today this area is occupied by the graves of local civilians, but in November 1863 this area was open and free from any graves.

In the many newspaper accounts of the dedication we can gleam clues as to the platform's location. The "Indianapolis Daily Journal" stated that "the great surging crowd around the stand . . . spreading down the slope almost to the line of the graves." This account by itself contradicts Mr. Selleck's location for he places the platform down the hill, beyond the graves. The same article continued by saying the platform stood, "nearly on the line of the diameter across the semi-circle of the cemetery, and the crowd filled the interior."

The distance from the Soldiers' National Monument "down the slope" to the graves is about 150 feet. The crowd at the dedication was estimated at 15,000 people. Could the space from the monument to the graves be adequate to hold such a large mass of people? Granted there would be less graves on November 19th than today. Only ⅓ of the dead had been transferred from the battlefield and hospital grave sites to the National Cemetery, 1,258 by the 19th; still the space was limited. The crowd was "to occupy the area in front of the stand, the military leaving sufficient space between them and the line of graves for the procession to pass." The officials of the dedication were very concerned that the fresh graves of the honored dead would not be desecrated by the tramping of the ensuing crowd. With Mr. Selleck's location, the crowd would be stepping

Frank Leslie's Sketch of the Soldiers' National Cemetery Dedication—Joseph Becker, artist for "Frank Leslie's Illustrated Newspaper" drew this detailed sketch of the dedication scene. The Cemetery Gatehouse #1 is prominent in the picture, with the platform #2 and Edward Everett's personal tent #3, beyond. Notice that the flag pole #4 is to the right (northwest) of the platform. To the far right you can see numerous grave markers #5, which would be the two eastern unknown sections.

on the graves because as the photographs reveal the crowd encircled the platform. The photographs of the dedication also reveal that there was a large open area in the rear of the crowd, separating them from the first row of graves. Only if the platform was moved farther up the hill into the grounds of the local cemetery would enough space be available to accommodate the huge crowd and preserve the sanctity of the graves.

The "National Intelligencer" said the scene was ". . . a grand and imposing one. The battlefield lay like a panorama in full view." The reporter for the "Philadelphia Daily Evening Bulletin" mentioned that he could see the Round Tops in the distance. The "Associated Press" accounts said the platform was "located at the highest point of ground on which the battle was fought." These witnesses plus others all indicate that the platform had to be near the crest of the hill, and the crest is located in the Evergreen Cemetery. The reporter of the "Cincinnati Daily Commercial" was very detailed in his account, stating that where the flag pole was raised, "it is proposed to erect a national monument," the present National Soldiers' Monument.

Taking all these accounts together, lends support that the platform was farther up the hill east of where the Soldiers' National Monument now stands. Also the visual evidence, Leslie's sketch and the photographs taken that November day, all show the platform nearer the crest of the hill, and thus located within the Evergreen Cemetery.

Only one object still exists that can be observed in the photographs; the arch gatehouse of the Evergreen Cemetery. This gatehouse is therefore the key and the reference point from which to interpret and determine the platform's location.

View from Gatehouse—This photograph was taken from the second story window of the Gatehouse. It shows the crowd gathering for the services, walking through the grounds of the local cemetery. Some of the grave stones in the photograph can be located today. To the right can be seen the rows of unknown soldier graves with their upright wooden markers. In the distance is the raised platform already crowded with dignitaries. Faintly to the right of the platform you can distinguish the flag pole, where the Soldiers' National Monument is standing today. In the photograph you are looking at the platform's side, which was 12 feet wide. Roughly measuring the distance between the platform and the flag pole the distance is about 25 yards.

Modern View from the second story window of the Gatehouse. To the right can be seen the Soldiers' National Monument where the flag pole stood that 19th of November.

This photograph was taken from the opposite side of the Cemetery looking toward the Gatehouse (marked by the left arrow) the right arrow marks the dedication platform, with the special tent pitched for the personal use of Edward Everett. Note the flag pole is to the left in this photograph.

Modern view looking toward the Gatehouse (left arrow) with the Soldiers' National Monument to the left. The dedication platform was about 25 yards from the Soldiers' Monument within the boundary of the local cemetery near the area marked by the right arrow.

This is part of the original sketch which was drawn by Joseph Becker before the scene was prepared more elaborately for Leslie's weekly. The soldiers' graves and flag pole are to the right, the gatehouse to the left while the platform is sketched in the rear center. (note the direction the platform is facing, toward the first section of soldier graves not directly toward the flag pole.) The arrow is pointing to a small obelisk gravestone. This gravestone can be located today in the local Evergreen Cemetery, marked by the arrow in the modern view. The speakers platform was located just behind and to the right of this obelisk gravestone very near the present iron fence separating the two cemeteries.
(Joseph Becker Collection, Terence J. Gallagher, U.S.A.M.H.I.)

Aerial view of the National Cemetery, showing the semicircular Civil War burial plots and the Soldier's National Monument in the center of the semi-circle. (NPS)

The Union Burial Plots

The Union graves form a large semicircle, with each of the eighteen states that contributed troops to the battle, having a designated plot. This semicircular design of William Saunders was conceived to maintain equality between all the soldiers and the states. The struggle of the Civil War was to preserve the Union, while the Gettysburg National Cemetery's design emphasizes the concept of States Rights. Within the burial plots there are 2 lieutenant-colonels, 2 majors, 11 captains, 56 lieutenants, 246 sergeants, 271 corporals, 1,362 privates, 5 musicians, 1 saddler, 1 chaplain, 4 women, 1 brevet major general, and 1,674 unknowns, all resting side by side: equal in burial. Reposing also in equality are men originally from many nations, including Ireland, England, Germany, Italy, Canada, as well as one Black American and one Native American.

The Gettysburg National Cemetery was established as a final resting place for those "Union" soldiers who gave their lives at Gettysburg. The Confederate dead were not given the honor of resting in these sacred grounds. Their graves were mostly mass graves scattered over the fields of battle, until 1872 when their badly decomposed bodies were disinterred and transported to southern cemeteries, such as Hollywood Cemetery in Richmond, Virginia. The person in charge of the exhumation of the Union bodies from the battlefield and hospital sites was the same Samuel Weaver referred to in the previous chapters. He made the following statement in his report: ". . . and I have most conscientiously assert, that I firmly believe that there has not been a single mistake made in the removal of the soldiers to the Cemetery by taking the body of a rebel for a Union soldier."[37] Oh, how wrong his statement was! As of this writing, nine Confederate soldiers have been located resting beside their Union counterparts: one in the Maryland plot, two in the plot of Massachusetts, two in the plot of Connecticut, and four in the Pennsylvania plot. There are probably others buried in the unknown plots that will never be discovered. These nine known Confederates may have fought under a different flag, but they deserve the same honor and tribute as all the Americans buried within the Gettysburg National Cemetery.

In this guide we will move clock-wise around the semicircle to each state plot. There are a total of 3,636 individuals buried within the semicircular section. Each person resting in these grounds is worthy of mention, but space limits us to only a few. Tribute however is given to all who are buried in this Cemetery.

The four years of the American Civil War witnessed the deaths of 622,000 Americans—the bloodiest conflict of our history. It can be stated with assurance that every family of the country was touched in some measure by the war, some more tragically than others. We hope that the stories which follow will touch the cords of your heart and awaken within your soul an "increased devotion to that cause for which they gave the last full measure of devotion."

Each row of the different state plots is assigned a letter. The outer most row being "A," the next row inward being "B," the next row inward "C" and so forth. An individual's grave can be located by counting from right to left in the designated row until you come to the number which that person has been assigned in this guide.

We ask that you not walk on the grave stones. Since they were first carved in 1864–65, they have undergone considerable wear.

U.S. Regulars Plot

Within this burial plot are those soldiers of the Regular Army. The majority of the men who served during the Civil War were volunteers in state regiments. But there were also some units which had existed before the war as part of the U.S. Army, referred to as Regulars.

Lieutenant Silas A. Miller
Company A 12th U.S. Infantry
Row D, #1

On July 18th, 1863 the Adjutant of the 12th U.S. Lieutenant Mimmack wrote to Charles Miller, the brother of the soldier resting in this grave: ". . . it is my painful duty to inform you that the report is perfectly true, that your brother was killed by a musket ball on July 2nd near Gettysburg, Pa.: His body was recovered from the field and buried the same night."

Lieutenant Mimmack continued, adding details of the death of Lieutenant Miller.

> The Regt. went into action about 5 p.m. July 2nd, and was under a very severe fire for some time from the enemy's sharpshooters. I think your brother must have been hit, about 6 p.m. He was shot through the body, near the heart—said, Oh! God, I am shot.—was moved to a rock near and only lived about ten minutes, he spoke no more, was unable, & evidently expected death, he seemed free from pain, nothing could be done for him of any avail. He died on the field, gallantly doing his duty. . . . He was buried at 10 p.m. on July 2nd in the enclosure of the nearest log house (J. Weikert) to the field on the side road (Wheatfield Road) near Sugar Loaf Hill (Little Round Top) seventeen paces southwest of house, on side of stone fence nr. pear tree. A board was put up at the head of the grave, marked with name & c and a small book with his name written on several pages, buried on his person. . . . His brother officers desired me to convey to his family, the

sincere condolence of the Regt. in the loss they have sustained."[38]

The loss sustained was severe, in that Lieutenant Silas Miller's family consisted of his three daughters: Ella Chandler age 11 (born June 4, 1852), Emma Louise age 9 (born June 5, 1854), and Annie Walsh age 6 (born Oct. 21, 1856). His wife of 11 years, Margaret Purdy had tragically died March 18, 1861, one month before the war began.

Within five months after his wife's death, to financially provide for his three daughters, Silas enlisted as a private in the 12th U.S. Infantry at $12.00 a month. He rose through the ranks, was commissioned a 2nd Lieutenant on Feb. 19, 1863 and a 1st Lieutenant one month before his death at Gettysburg. As a Lieutenant he received a monthly pay of $105.50.

With their father serving in the army, the three girls lived with their grandfather, Silas Miller Sr. and their uncle Charles Miller at Piermont, New York. We can only imagine the grief, the emotional trauma and depression that the girls suffered with the loss of their father so soon after the loss of their mother. Their emotional state could partly explain what happened early the next year. The oldest daughter, Ella, mysteriously died on February 24th, with the youngest girl, Annie, dying a month later on March 31st. Emma, the middle aged girl was diagnosed with epilepsy. Tragedy again stalked the Miller family when the grandfather passed away in July of 1865. Annie Miller passed away unmarried, on August 22, 1903 at the age of 49.

Private Dennis Wallace
5th U.S. Artillery, Battery I
Row D #16

During the fierce struggle on the slopes of Little Round Top, the afternoon of July 2nd, Battery I, 5th U.S. Artillery was literally heaved and dragged with abundant sweat to the hill's crest. "The passage of the guns through the roadless woods and amongst the rocks was marvelous," explained General Henry Hunt. From the hill's heights the guns thundered forth against the attacking enemy's lines.

The bugler of the battery was 27 year old Irish born Dennis Wallace. A Confederate shell exploded beneath him, splintering both his legs. He was carried to the rear where both legs were amputated just below his hip. Lieutenant Benjamin F. Rittenhouse, commander of the Battery, relates that on July 4th, while he was visiting the wounded he came upon Private Wallace. "The surgeons were probing for a ball in the sergeant's leg (a sergeant that was lying next to Wallace), and he was making considerable fuss. The little bugler (Dennis Wallace) grew impatient, and sung out, 'Stop your noise, what is the use of making such a devil of a racket. I don't make any fuss, and I have been trimmed down until I am not as long as a yard stick.' "[39]

Private Wallace suffered from his horrible wounds for another month, dying in the Camp Letterman Hospital on August 2nd. He left behind in Marlborrough, Massachusetts his wife Abby Delia Dunn (they were married August 7, 1853) and his 7 year old son, Thomas, born April 25, 1855.

Private Henry Gooden
127th U.S. Colored Troops
Row D #30

During the war, blacks served mostly as wagon drivers, cooks, servants and laborers. However there were several black regiments that performed heroically in combat. There were no black regiments in the battle of Gettysburg. Of the nearly 200,000 black American soldiers and sailors serving the Union cause, over 8,000 gave their lives and 21 received our country's highest award of valor, the Medal of Honor.

Henry Gooden is the only black soldier of the Civil War buried within this National Cemetery. He enlisted in the 127th U.S. Colored Infantry on August 26, 1864 at Carlisle, Pennsylvania. His enlistment records tells us that he was 5 feet 3 inches in height, a laborer by occupation and age 43. He saw limited enemy action, spending most of his one year enlistment guarding military posts and herding cattle for the army in Texas. He returned to Carlisle, where he died August 15, 1876. There are numerous others buried within the semicircle plots that are not casualties of the Gettysburg battle, but were buried years after the war as veterans.

Lieutenant Wesley F. Miller
Company E, 7th U.S. Infantry
Row D #29

The body of Lieutenant Wesley Miller was removed from this grave supposedly by family members, years after the National Cemetery was dedicated, and reburied 35 miles north of Gettysburg within the Harrisburg City Cemetery. Today his grave in Harrisburg is marked by a worn and broken headstone.

Co-author James Cole standing by the broken headstone of Lieut. Wesley Miller's grave in Harrisburg City Cemetery.

Lieutenant Miller was 20 years of age when he was killed July 2nd on Houck's Ridge near the Wheatfield. He was the eldest son of Maragret and Stephen Miller of St. Cloud, Minnesota. He along with his father had enlisted at Fort Snelling into Company D of the 1st Minnesota Regiment only two weeks after the bombardment and surrender of Fort Sumter. Because of his political connections the father, Stephen Miller was chosen to be the Lieut-Colonel of the regiment. He led a section of the unit in the fierce fighting on Henry House Hill during the battle of First Manassas, then later led the 7th Minnesota as its Colonel and was in charge of the execution of 38 Sioux Indians who had attacked white settlements in Minnesota during the summer of 1862. In the election of 1863, he was elected Governor of the state, serving until January 8, 1866. He died in Worthington, Minnesota August 19, 1881.

Lieutenant Miller served in the 1st Minnesota until he received a Lieutenant's commission in the 7th U.S. Infantry on December 7th, 1861. He served in this regular regiment until his death at Gettysburg.

On July 20th, 1863, Wesley's father wrote to a young woman he greeted as "My Dear Mary," who we judge from the letter to be Wesley's fiance. Part of the letter read as follows:

". . . I suppose that the relations between you and he (Wesley) were quite intimate. I did not think that they had so fully matured. I need not say that you would have been very dear to me as a daughter, and that had Wesley lived I should always have said that he was unworthy of you; and you shall be none the less dear to me now that he has departed.

"Poor lad! He had his failings but was a youth of noble impulses.

"It is hard to find substantial comfort for such a terrible loss: but we have this consolation at least that he died battling for the best government upon Earth, and in the holiest causes ever vindicated by warriors upon the field of slaughter. Better that all my children and their father too—should fall, than that the old flag should trail in the dust, or one star be erased from its field of light."[40]

Maryland Plot

The loyalty of the State of Maryland was critical to the survival of the Federal Government, seeing that Washington was bordered by the state. Maryland was deeply divided in its loyalties. Parts of the state were solidly pro-Union while other areas, such as the city of Baltimore, were teeming with secessionists. Early in the war, President Lincoln arrested and jailed a large number of the state's congressmen to ensure that the legislature would not vote to secede from the Union.

At Gettysburg, regiments from Maryland served in both armies, even fighting opposite one another on the wooded slopes of Culp's Hill. It is therefore appropriate that one of the nine known Confederate soldiers buried within the Cemetery would be from Maryland, resting beside his fellow Marylanders who had fought on the Union side.

Private Ninion F. Knott
Company F, 2nd Maryland Battalion CSA
Row C #4

Little at the present time is known of Private Knott, except that he was from Baltimore. He was mortally wounded during the fierce fighting on Culp's Hill the morning of July 3rd, a bullet striking him in the left side and exiting near the spine. He died August 24th.

Private George Henry Barger
Co. H 1st Maryland Potomac Home Brigade
Row B #2

A genealogical historian must use many tools to piece together the puzzles of those lives of the past: newspapers, census, military files, county records, family lore, etc. One invaluable resource are the pension files of the Federal Government available in the National Archives at Washington, D.C.

On July 14, 1862 the United States Congress passed an act that granted pensions to the dependents of those soldiers and sailors who died during the war. Those dependents included widows, minor children, and parents. However extensive documentation was required to prove that the claimants had truly been dependent financially upon the deceased serviceman. Within the pension files you discover a microcosm of the lives of these families: birth, marriage, death records, medical histories, depositions, letters from the soldiers, and even at times soldiers' diaries. You also discover that an extra $8.00 to $12.00 a month from the government can cause the evil monster of greed to grow, causing individuals to lie and fight within their own families for the extra money. The overwhelming majority of those applying for the pensions deserved and needed them, many being destitute from the loss of their loved ones. However, on occasion a file emerges which makes you shake your head and declare, "do they really think the government is going to buy this story?" One such case is the following.

Private George H. Barger at the age of 30 was killed in the Union counter-attack upon Culp's Hill the morning of July 3rd. His death left 3 orphaned children in Berlin, Maryland: Charles age 7, Theophilris age 5 and a step-daughter Martha. His wife Mary Elizabeth Grove (she was previously married, widowed in 1853, and had married George Barger April 24, 1855 at Frederick, Maryland) had died February 19, 1862. The grandmother, Mahala Barger became the children's guardian and rightfully received the pension for the two boys, up to their 16th birthdays.

The trouble arises 42 years later in 1905. The two boys, now men, 50 and 47 years of age, wrote extensive and numerous depositions to the Federal Pension Office claiming that the government owed them money that originally had been owed to their father. They claimed the government owed $55.57 in back pay to their father, plus interest, $45.00 on a bounty, plus interest, and $350.53½ plus in-

terest for pension money due them as "minor children" of Priv. Barger. The government duly rejected the obvious fraudulent claim.[41]

Row upon row of the individually numbered headstones of the unknown, numbering up to 979.

Unknown Plot #1

As stated earlier, Samuel Weaver was unable to identify the state designation of 979 of the bodies he disinterred from the battlefield. However several of these "total unknowns" were in reality known by name, but the state they served from could not be ascertained. He could not bury these bodies in a state plot, so therefore these men suffered the fate of being laid to their rest in an unknown grave. Thankfully, Weaver recorded in his notes the stone number of each of these men.

Sergeant Cyrus Melville Hall
Company B 17th Maine Infantry
Stone #598

Shortly after the battle, Emma Norris Hall, age 23, received the notice of the death of her husband, Sergeant Cyrus Hall. The letter said that he was "killed the 3rd of July while we (17th Maine) were supporting a battery. A shell burst between him and Munroe Quint (he is buried in the Maine plot, Row D, grave #11) killing them both and wounding George L. Dunan, James McKean and Lieutenant Greene of Co. B. Your husband's loss is a heavy blow for us, for he was possessed of so many good qualities."[4]

Emma and Sergeant Hall were married on June 14, 1862 in Portland, Maine. They had only one child, born March 18, 1863. Sergeant Hall of course was at the front when his son was born, but he had asked his wife to name their boy, Willie Melville Hall.

In two years the young widow would remarry, to Melvin Marston and officially have her son's first name dropped, stating that she had never liked the name of "Willie."[42]

Private William Martin
Company K, 134th New York Infantry
Stone #608

The 134th New York, part of Coster's Brigade of the 11th Corps, took severe casualties the afternoon of July 1st in a brickyard along North Stratton Street. William Martin was one who was killed that day. He was 42 years of age from Niskayuna, New York.

Private Martin and his wife, Elizabeth West Martin, (married December 10, 1843) had four children: John Henry (born February 25, 1851), Charles L. (born April 18, 1854), Francis E. (born Sept. 5, 1860), and Alida J. (born January 13, 1863). Its their little girl that makes this soldier's story so compelling. Alida was born severely mentally and physically handicapped. The testimony claims that she acted like a "wild creature," totally dependent upon others. So often during that period of time, people who were mentally retarded were locked up and forgotten by their families and society. It is therefore a credit to Elizabeth Martin and her family that they choose to care for Alida, even after the loss of her husband. By 1910 Alida was 47 years of age, and was living with her older sister Francis, in Schenectady, New York. On October 25 of that year, an unexplained accident occurred. Stored kerosene oil cans exploded, killing Alida, who for reasons unknown, was playing among them. She was buried in the family plot of the Reformed Dutch Church Cemetery at Niskayuna, New York.[43]

Indiana Plot

Private John E. Weaver
Company A, 3rd Indiana Cavalry
Row C, #6

On the early morning of July 1st, the Confederate Division of Major General Harry Heth approached the town of Gettysburg from the west not expecting any stiff resistance from the thin line of Union cavalry that stood before them. However, the Union cavalry was commanded by a highly capable officer, Brigadier General John Buford. His troopers stubbornly delayed the Confederate advance, enabling the Union First Corps to be rushed forward initiating the greatest battle ever to be waged on American soil.

One of these troopers was Private John E. Weaver, of the 3rd Indiana Cavalry, who has the distinction of being the first Union casualty of the battle. Weaver enlisted on February 24, 1862 at Vevay, Indiana. His military service record tells us that he was 21 years of age when he enlisted, was 5 feet 10 inches tall, of fair complexion and that his civilian occupation had been a wagon maker.

During the early morning fighting, a Confederate shell exploded close to him, a large shrapnal ball tearing into the bone of his left leg. His horse was also struck, dying on the spot. Weaver was carried to the rear where his leg was amputated. As in many cases when amputation occurred, infection developed and Weaver died August 3rd. The bone from his severed leg was preserved and kept for medical study. It is today in the collection of the Armed Forces Institute of Pathology, located at Walter Reed Hospital, Washington.

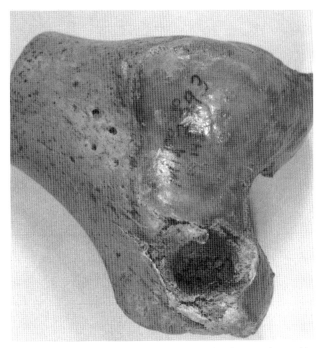

The leg bone of Priv. John Weaver, clearly showing the wound caused by a case-shot ball. (Armed Forces Institute of Pathology, Walter Reed Hospital, Washington, D.C.)

Row E, #9

The listing of burials reveals that the soldier buried here belonged to Company K of the 27th Indiana Regiment. This was possibly determined by the soldier's uniform, in that they would at times have their company and regimental designation on their hats. Seven men of Company K, 27th Indiana would die as a result of the regiment's action in Spangler's Meadow the morning of July 3rd. The burial sites of five of the seven can be determined, therefore by the process of elimination the soldier buried in this grave should be either Sergeant Conrad Mehne or Private William D. Monroe.

Sergeant Conrad Mehne lived in Hayesville, Dubois County, Indiana. He was married to Elizabeth Frank on November 6, 1856. They had two boys: John (born September 30, 1858), and Conrad Jr. (born October 28, 1861).

Private William D. Monroe was single, from Hamilton County, Indiana. He however would send most of his military pay as support to his 12 year old sister, Mary Jane Monroe, as their parents had died shortly before the war.

Ohio Plot

Sergeant Philip Tracy
Company G, 8th Ohio Infantry
Row B, #22

Philip Tracy was young, merely 17, when he married his sweetheart, Susannah Pymer in 1856. The young couple looked forward in raptured anticipation of becoming parents, as the birth of their first child approached in the first month of 1857. Their son, William was born on January 12th. However the delivery was too strenuous for the young Susannah to bear, she died one month later on February 11th.

Philip was devastated, the love of his life was gone forever. But a new life needed to be loved and nurtured. With the assistance of Susannah's mother, Catharine, Philip Tracy began the difficult yet rewarding task of raising and guiding his little boy. The relationship between father and son lovingly grew.

In the summer of 1861, Philip enlisted in the 8th Ohio Regiment, for reasons only he knew. Little William, now 5 years old, would shed tears at being separated from his father, but knowing kids, those tears were certainly mixed with youthful pride as his father marched off in the uniform of blue.

The 8th Ohio was a critical unit in the repulse of the Confederate attack against the Union center on July 3rd. The Regiment was in an advanced position beyond the Emmitsburg Road, giving it the perfect opportunity to strike the left flank of the Confederate assault. The entire Confederate Brigade of Colonel Brockenbrough's had dissolved and was fleeing to the rear. The Ohioans continued to rake the left units of the Confederate line, gathering in numerous prisoners and enemy flags. Sergeant Tracy, heroically leading his company, received a musket bullet in his shoulder. He would die of this wound on July 5th.[44]

The war had taken 7 year old William Tracy's most cherished object, his father.

Private George Nixon
Company B, 73rd Ohio Infantry
Row C, #4

There are a few graves in the Cemetery that are repeatedly pointed to by Park Rangers and Battlefield Guides.

Priv. George Nixon, 73rd Ohio Inf. (Julie Nixon Eisenhower)

One of these is the grave of George Nixon, who was the great grandfather of the 37th President of the United States, Richard M. Nixon.

George Nixon was born in Washington County, Pennsylvania in 1821. On June 10, 1843, he was united in marriage to Margret Ann Trimmer, and soon afterwards moved to Ohio. Their marriage saw nine children born: their third child, Samuel Brady Nixon, born in 1847 would be the grandfather of the future President.

George enlisted at Waverly, Ohio in the 73rd Regiment of the state, December 30, 1861, at the age of 40. He was 5 feet 6 inches in height and listed his civilian occupation as a farmer.

During the fighting at Gettysburg, the 73rd Ohio was on skirmish duty along and beyond the Emmitsburg Road at the outskirts of town. The 73rd Ohio's regimental monument lies just beyond the Cemetery wall to your west. During the hot skirmishing of the second day, Private Nixon received a wound in his hip. "His moans and cries for help could be heard distinctly by his comrades across the intervening wheatfield."[45] As darkness fell, a 19 year old drummer of the regiment, Richard Enderlin, decided he would brave an attempt to rescue the wounded Private Nixon.

"Enderlin stripped himself of arms and superfluous clothing, and proceeded to crawl upon his face over the intervening space, taking advantage as he could of the occasional darkness, as the clouds obscured the moon. By slow and cautious movement he at length reached the side of the wounded man, whispered his presence and purpose . . . succeeding in getting Nixon on his back and then began slowly to crawl toward the Union line. All this time, over and about him the picket firing was constant.''[46]

As Enderlin neared the Union lines he made a mad dash for safety. For this heroic deed Enderlin was awarded the Medal of Honor. The wound received by Nixon proved fatal. He died July 14th.

The tragic story of George Nixon does not end at Gettysburg, for his beloved wife, Margret would die less than two years later, March 19, 1865, leaving their large family as orphans.

Then Vice-President, Richard Nixon (second from right) placing flowers on the grave of his great grand father George Nixon in 1956. (NPS)

Private Haskell Farr
Company G, 55th Ohio Infantry
Row E, #6

At the age of 18, Haskell Farr had enlisted in the 55th Ohio at Republic, Ohio. He was 5 feet, 10 inches in height, had hazel colored eyes, red hair and had been a farmer.

The 55th Ohio was positioned at the northwestern base of Cemetery Hill. Farr was mortally wounded during the skirmishing of July 2nd near the Dobbin House. In many cases, wounded soldiers would show signs of improvement, only to develop infection or hemorrhaging. This was the case with Private Farr. He died in the army hospital at Gettysburg November 19th, the very day President Lincoln would stand within a few yards of this spot to dedicate these grounds ''as a final resting place for those who here gave their lives that that nation might live.''

Massachusetts Plot

Corporal Michael O'Laughlin
Company K, 13th Massachusetts Infantry
Row A, #33

Sergeant Austin Stearns of the 13th Massachusetts related:

"In the afternoon while (I was) in the church (Christ Lutheran) with the boys the surgeons came around to make an examination of Mike O'Laughlin ('s) wound; he was shot through the knee (left knee) and the bone was badly smashed. They gave it a pretty thorough looking over, and concluded it must be taken off. Mike cried like a baby when the surgeons made their decision and plead his poverty and an aged Mother that was dependent on him as a reason why he could not part (with) it. I pitied him, as did all the surgeons, and they promised to wait a few days before taking it off, but poor Mike, he lost his limb and his life as well.''[47]

Michael O'Laughlin lingered until October 8th, dying at the age of 21. O'Laughlin was born in Galway, Ireland, immigrating to America with his parents when he was a small boy. The family settled in Strewsberry, Massachusetts, where Michael labored as a shoemaker.

Lying wounded in Christ Lutheran Church at Gettysburg, he had pleaded for his leg because of his ''aged mother,'' Margret, who was 'dependent on him.'' His father, Patrick O'Laughlin, had died several years earlier, leaving Michael as the chief provider of the family. Mrs. O'Laughlin received $12.00 a month pension from the Federal Government and $1.00 a week pension from the State of Massachusetts until her death several years later.[48]

Private Edwin Field
Company B, 13th Massachusetts Infantry
Row A, #34

During the fighting of July 1st, Private Edwin Field was shot in his left lung and carried into Gettysburg to Christ Lutheran Church, which was being utilized as a hospital.

Private Field was born in Chelsea, Massachusetts June 30, 1841. He was the youngest in the family of Charles and Mary Field. (They were married August 5, 1822) His one brother, George was age 16, and his two sisters, Mary Ann age 14 and Susan age 9 when he was born.

Private Field enlisted and was mustered into the 13th Massachusetts on July 17, 1861. During his enlistment, he wrote numerous letters to his parents and his oldest sister, who had married Edward Chapman in 1848. Several of these letters are preserved in Edwin Field's pension file at the National Archives.[49]

In these letters, Private Field talks about the news of the war, stating once that ''. . . more battle before this war will be closed.''

He also regularly sent money back home to his parents and sister, and repeatedly thanked his family for the gifts and packages, especially the postage stamps. "I was very glad that Edward (Mary Ann's husband) is going to send me some gray underclothing. White is not fit for a soldier to wear as it so much trouble to keep them clean."

In one letter to his sister he mentions that "mother" had written, that she was terribly worried about his health. ". . . you tell mother when I get low spirited it will be time to write, as long as my health is as good as it is. I known she need not be afraid of my being low spirited. I never was in better spirits in my life, than I am now. I feel strong and hearty. I have never regretted that I joined the army to fight in so glorious a cause."[10]

Private Edwin Field died of his chest wound on July 3rd. He had written months before, "PS, Remember me to all my many friends."[51]

Priv. Edwin Field, 13th Massachusetts. (Scott Hann)

Private John Fly
Company K, 13th Massachusetts Infantry
Row A, #38

During the retreat of the Union forces through the streets of Gettysburg the afternoon of July 1st, Private Austin Stearns of the 13th Massachusetts had taken refuge in Christ Lutheran Church posing as a medical assistant. During the morning of July 2nd, while walking along Chambersburg Street, he happened to be at the right place at the right time.

"On going back towards the church I saw a rebel ambulance standing before the door with several of our Surgeons standing besides it earnestly talking. On getting near I heard they were talking about some one in the ambulance. On looking in I saw there, dressed in a rebel uniform and very weak from the loss of blood, John Flye, the first man of our company hit. I told the surgeons that I knew that man, that we were of the same company, and they immediately ordered him to be taken in. Flye was left on the field, and the rebs finding him, and seeing his clothes covered and growing stiff with blood, had exchanged his pants for one of their own, and brought him in. The surgeons, seeing him in gray, could not believe he was a Union soldier."[52]

If Private Fly's comrade had not identified him in the street, he could have been buried as a Confederate soldier and thus his remains would have been carried south seven years later to be buried. Truly this story is remarkable, but allow us to add to its uniqueness.

Private John Fly was 31 and in civilian life had been a blacksmith in Westborough, Massachusetts. He had married Harriet Copeland on May 6, 1860, she being age 23. Upon receiving word of the wounding of her husband, Harriet rushed to Gettysburg and was at his side when he died on July 27th. On February 15, 1864, she applied to the War Department in Washington for the pension of her deceased husband. Her application was denied, due to the fact that the pension had already been claimed by another Mrs. Fly. Harriet was shocked to learn that her husband had been previously married.

On January 7, 1849 in Augusta, Maine, John Fly had married Rachael Jane Bragg. They had one child, John Fly Jr., born April 9, 1850. The marriage had failed and John and Rachael divorced on May 13, 1857. When he married Harriet in 1860, John choose not to mention his former wife nor the fact that he had a son. Needless to say, Harriet was aghast at the revelation.

She tried to build her case for the pension, even gathering suspective evidence that the former Mrs. Fly had committed bigamy in marrying her present husband, William Brock, and that she had been involved in prostitution while married to Private Fly. The pension however was not in Rachael's name but in the name of the minor son, John Fly Jr. age 14. Thus the War Department ruled that Harriet Fly had no legal claim to the pension.[53]

Private Jeremiah Danforth
Company C, 19th Massachusetts Infantry

Private Charles A. Trask
Private Charles H. Wellington
Company K, 13th Massachusetts Infantry
Row D, #29, #30, & #31

The three individuals buried in these plots were not casualties of the Gettysburg battle, in fact when the battle raged over these fields, these three soldiers were already dead for nearly a year.

While the Battle of Gettysburg was the bloodiest battle of the Civil War, 51,000 casualties over three days, the battle of Antietam, Maryland, fought on September 17th 1862 was the bloodiest single day of the war and of our country's history with 26,000 casualties. These three soldiers were mortally wounded at Antietam in the savage fighting in and around the Cornfield. They were transported to a hospital in Chambersburg, Pennsylvania (only 25 miles west of Gettysburg), where Private Wellington died on October 1st, Private Trask the next day, and Private Danforth on October 5th.

Private Trask was from Banger, Maine, a shoemaker by trade. He was 20 years old when he died.[54] Private Wellington was 23 years of age from Holden, Massachusetts and was also a shoemaker in civilian life. Private Danforth was 43 years of age when he enlisted with his 19 year old son, George on August 29, 1861. (George was wounded during the battle of Fredericksburg and was mustered out of Federal service August 29, 1864.)

Three days before Jeremiah died he wrote the following letter through his nurse, to his wife Abigail in Massachusetts.

> "I thought I would take this opportunity to inform you that on account of being wounded and my health being very poor, I am in the hospital here. (Chambersburg) It will please you to know that I am well taken care of, and only want to see you and our dear children again. There is nothing that the people here have that they do not bring in for us—they come and ask me what I will have to eat, and bring me whatever I want. My appetite is very poor, and my wound painful. I should have written before, but had no paper or pen, and was not well enough acquainted with any one here to ask them to write for me. I want you and Julia (his 16 year old daughter) and all the rest to write soon, and send me some envelopes and postage stamps. I have not heard from George, but got a man to write to him yesterday. If I ever get well—and I am afraid I will not—I shall not stay in the army any longer.
>
> "Our regiment was very badly cut up—I suppose you have read the newspaper accounts of the battle. I have not heard a word from any one in the regiment since the battle.
>
> "Give my love and best respects to all my friends and ask them to write to me as soon as they can. I am here now, but it is uncertain how long I shall stay here, and unless you write immediately, I may miss your letter. Direct your letters to Chambersburg, Pa."[55]

The day after his death, the same nurse who had written the first letter wrote to his wife: ". . . Yesterday—on Sabbath afternoon between 4 and 5 o'clock Mr. Danforth's sufferings on earth was over. . . . Your husband remarked to me that he had seen many kind faces here and many good familiar actions, which reminded him of home—'Indeed' he said, 'if it had not been for that, I do not believe I could have kept up as long as I have.' "

The officials of the State of Massachusetts had been in the forefront in the establishment of the Gettysburg Soldiers' Cemetery, insisting that all known soldiers be buried in state plots rather than randomly. Therefore the bodies of Privates Trask, Wellington, and Danforth were transferred from their grave sites in Chambersburg to be reunited with their Massachusetts comrades. They are the only soldiers buried in the Civil War section who were fatal battle casualties from a campaign other than Gettysburg.

Lieut. Sumner Paine, Co. A, 20th Massachusetts Infantry buried in Row E, grave #1 of the Massachusetts Section. Lieut. Paine was only 18 years of age when he was killed by a shell fragment on July 3rd.

Confederates from Mississippi
Private John T. Johnson
Company K, 11th Mississippi Infantry
Row C, #1

Private Johnson was a student from Carrollton, Mississippi, enlisting in the Confederate service on March 8, 1862, at the age of 18. He was mortally wounded as his regiment (one of the units of General Joseph Davis' Brigade) attempted to storm the stonewall at the Union center on Cemetery Ridge July 3rd. He died of his wound on August 4th at the General Hospital, Camp Letterman. He was buried in the hospital cemetery as a Confederate soldier. After several months when the burial detail began to transfer the bodies from the Letterman Hospital graveyard, many of the wooden headboards were difficult to read due to weathering from the elements. This is probably the reason why the Confederates were mistakenly buried in the National Cemetery. In the case of Private Johnson and the other Confederate buried in the Massachusetts section, the abbreviation for Mississippi was mistakenly read as Massachusetts.

Private N. B. Hindman
Company A, 13th Mississippi Infantry
Row E, #8

This Confederate soldier enlisted in the Winston Guards on May 23, 1861 at Corinth, Mississippi, age 22. He was a single farmer from Lewisville, Georgia. Private Hindman spent the time of his enlistment as a wagon driver, staying in the rear, until the Gettysburg battle. He was pressed into the front ranks—his first and last time as a combat soldier. The 13th Mississippi was the right regiment of the Brigade of General William Barksdale. Near 6:00 p.m. on July 2nd, Barksdale's Brigade overwhelmed the advanced and exposed Union position in the Peach Orchard along the Emmitsburg Road. The 13th Mississippi swept through the Orchard and confronted the guns of the 9th Massachusetts Bettery at the Trostle Farm, a quarter mile behind the Orchard. The Massachusetts Battery held their isolated position for over ten minutes firing at point blank range, before being overrun in hand-to-hand fighting. We do not know at what point in the struggle, that Private Hindman was wounded, but he was struck in the left lung. He died in the Federal hospital on August 14th.

Minnesota Plot

The urn memorial within the Minnesota Plot was erected in 1867 by the survivors of the 1st Minnesota Regiment in memory of their fallen comrades. This is the oldest monument on the Gettysburg battlefield. Inscribed upon this memorial is a brief part of Edward Everett's lengthy speech delivered November 19th, during the dedication services;

"All time is the millennium of their glory."

The 1st Minnesota Infantry Regiment made one of the most gallant charges of the battle. The late afternoon of July 2nd, the Confederates were sweeping the Union Third Corps back from its advanced position along the Emmitsburg Road. Victory was within the southern's grasp. The 1st Minnesota, about 262 men, was ordered to charge this overwhelming Confederate tide.

> "Every man realized in an instant what that order meant. Death or wounds to us all—the sacrifice of the regiment to gain a few minutes time and save the position and probably the battlefield, and every man saw and accepted the necessity for that sacrifice, and responding to Colvill's (Colonel of the Regiment) rapid orders, the regiment in perfect line, with arms at right shoulder shift was in a moment down that slope directly upon the enemy's center."[56]

The small number of Minnesotians fought heroically. Almost surrounded, they had gained the time needed so other Union units could be rushed into the defense. The 1st Minnesota had suffered greatly. Of the 262 men who made the gallant charge, only 47 were unscathed. The next day the remnant participated in the repulse of Pickett's Assault upon the Union center, losing 17 more men. The Regiment suffered a total casualty rate of 82% during the battle.

The oldest monument on the Gettysburg battlefield, the Minnesota Urn erected in 1867.

Captain Nathan S. Messick
Company G, 1st Minnesota Infantry
Row A, #4

There are many forgotten heroes of the Gettysburg battle. Lying in this grave is truly one of those forgotten heroes.

Captain Messick had enlisted at Fort Snelling, Minnesota on April 29, 1861 at the age of 34. During the battle of First Manassas (July 21, 1861) after the regiment's flag had received numerous bullet holes, he stripped the tattered banner from its staff and wrapped it around his body to protect it from any more damage.

In January of 1863, the regiment's assistant surgeon had declared Messick unfit for duty due to "chronic hepatitis." The medical officer was insistent, saying "to prevent permanent disability or loss of life," Captain Messick should be relieved from duty and sent home. Captain Messick accepted a month's furlough but refused to resign. He spent the month of February in Faribault, Minnesota in the loving care of his wife, Amanda and his four daughters (Mary W. age 13, Euphemia L. age 10, Lizzie A. age 5 and Georgia age 3). In early March, Captain Messick returned to the regiment's encampment in Virginia, even though he was still suffering from his illness.[57]

After the sacrificial charge the evening of July 2nd, Captain Messick was the highest ranking surviving officer. He took command of the gallant few of the regiment. The afternoon of July 3rd, General Lee launched his massive frontal attack upon the Union center, known as "Pickett's Charge." Sergeant James Wright of the 1st Minnesota related that the Confederate assault "was a magnificent spectacle. A rising tide of armed men rolling toward us in steel crested billows. It was an intensely interesting sight especially to us who must face it, brest it, break it,—or be broken by it."[58]

The Confederate tide moved ever forward, increasing its speed as it neared the Union lines. The Union ranks behind the stone wall on Cemetery Ridge fired volley upon murderous volley into the on-rushing wave of Pickett's men, but the wave broke over the wall and into the Union center. Union regiments were quickly shifted to counter, and drive the enemy back over that low wall. The remnant of the 1st Minnesota led by Captain Nathan Messick was one of those units that was rushed toward the crisis. While urging his men, Captain Messick was struck in the head by a shell fragment and instantly killed.

A personal friend of Captain Messick, Edward Bassnett, helped carry the lifeless body to the rear.

"We took him back to the Field Hospital where his cook took charge, staying with him until an ambulance took him to the General Hospital. His sword and pocket book were taken from him within fifteen minutes after he fell. Who took them, I don't know. There was perhaps $15.00 in it. . . . After we laid him down, I was looking at him for the last time, and thinking if there was anything more that I could do, that would do any good. I asked Mr. Williams,

his cook, to take off his shoulder straps and send to his wife, which he did. I am sorry that we couldn't save his sword, but in a battle like that there are lots of things one would like to do, but cannot. . . . He died at his post doing his duty. Thousands fell that day the same way. Captain Messick died as he would wish to die, fighting for his country."[59]

Capt. Nathan S. Messick, 1st Minnesota (Minnesota Historical Society)

Sergeant Philip R. Hamlin
Company F, 1st Minnesota Infantry
Row A, #10

Private James A. Wright related about the evening of July 3rd.

". . . as we drank our coffee we decided to bury Hamlin that night. Search was made for a spade and after some time a shovel was found. With this a shallow trench was dug beside a walnut tree, near which he had been killed, struck by four bullets. His blanket and tent-cloth were spread in it, he was then laid upon them and covered with the remaining portions. Then those present knelt in silence about him, with uncovered, bowed heads. I do not recall that a word was spoken; but it was a sincere and reverential service fitting the time and the situation. then we covered him over with the dirt and stones we had thrown out of the trench and placed at his head a board, on which his name, company and regiment, had been marked."[60]

Sergt. Philip R. Hamlin, 1st Minnesota. (Minnesota Historical Society)

Capt. Joseph Periam, 1st Minnesota (Minnesota Historical Society)

Sergeant Hamlin age 23, lived and labored on his parent's (Rice & Elizabeth Hamlin) farm at New Haven, Minnesota. His older brother, Jacob Leslie Hamlin, was a member of the 7th Minnesota Regiment and was mortally wounded in the battle of Nashville, Tennessee, December 1864.

Sergeant Hamlin was described by a fellow comrade as "always and everywhere an honest, earnest, consistent, Christian man; whose open unostentatious, frank, manly and unobtrusive observance of what he considered his religion, was well-known and respected by all who knew him."[61]

In one of his letters he instructed his father to "pay $1.00 to the preacher (Methodist-Episcopal) . . . I have resolved to devote $1.00 each pay to God."[62]

In another letter he wrote, "My trust is in God. During all the battle His grace sustainest me. In Him alone I am indebted for courage, strength and all else that is essential to a discharge of duty. Pray for me and our cause."

Captain Joseph Periam
Company K, 1st Minnesota Infantry
Row B, #9

Captain Periam was horribly wounded the evening of July 2nd when struck in the nose by a bullet, which penetrated through his skull, exiting behind the ear. He lingered until July 7th, dying at the age of 34.

Private Isaac L. Taylor
Company E, 1st Minnesota Infantry
Row B, #12

The stone reads "unknown," but buried in this grave is possibly Private Isaac Taylor. He enlisted in the 1st Minnesota Regiment at Fort Snelling, at the age of 24. During the battle of Savage Station, Virginia June 29, 1862, he received a wound in the shoulder and was taken prisoner. He was shortly afterwards paroled. Private Taylor was killed the evening of July 2nd during the regiment's counter-attack.

44

Priv. Isaac L. Taylor (right) with his brother Patrick, 1st Minnesota. (Minnesota Historical Society)

Connecticut Plot

Private Moses G. Clement
Company G, 14th Connecticut Infantry
Row A, #4

Moses Clement enlisted in the 14th Connecticut July 31st, 1862 from Guilford, Connecticut. His service record says he was 5 feet, 9½ inches in height, having dark hair and complexion, with gray eyes. He was 30 years of age and a farmer by trade.

Standing between Cemetery and Seminary Ridges was the house and farm buildings of William Bliss. These buildings had been repeatedly occupied by Confederates using them to snipe at the Union line only 400 yards distant. Likewise, Union units had repeatedly driven the Confederates snipers from the buildings and occupied them in return. Through the morning of July 3rd, the buildings were captured and recaptured three times by Union forces. Near 11:00 a.m. the under strength 14th Connecticut (a mere 160 men) had again taken the house and barn and would torch both structures. Confederate artillery commenced to rain shells upon the stone barn. One shell crashed through the northern gable and exploded within. Private Moses Clement was instantly killed. His brother, Sergeant Nathan Clement of the same company, gathered the personal effects from his brother's body, a silver watch and some money. These were sent to Moses' widow, Jane, in Guilford. They had been married December 5, 1858, but had no children.[64]

It should be noted that the brother, did not survive the war, dying of disease January of 1864. Jane Clement died in Vermont at the age of 53 in 1880.

Sergeant Aaron Greenwald
Company C, 1st Minnesota Infantry
Row C, #15

The headstone of this grave site reads, "unknown ordnance sergeant." The ordnance sergeant of the 1st Minnesota who was a casualty of the battle was Aaron Greenwald. He had survived the counter-attack of the regiment the evening of July 2nd only to receive a mortal wound during the fighting of the next day. He died of his wound three days later, at the age of 30. He left in Anoka, Minnesota his wife, Anne Sweeney Greenwald (married September 15, 1858) and his two young boys, William age 3½ and Louis John age 2½. If his sons ever visited Gettysburg seeking their father's grave, their search would have been fruitless, as the stone is marked "unknown."[63]

Private Daniel H. Purdy
Company C, 17th Connecticut Infantry
Row B, #6

On the afternoon of July 1st, the 17th Connecticut had the hapless honor of being positioned on the extreme right flank of the XI Corps exposed battle line. When the Confederate Brigade of Brig. Gen. John B. Gordon advanced against this right flank, the 17th Connecticut with bayonets fixed, counter-charged. Fierce hand-to-hand fighting ensued. The regiment was shattered by the Confederate onslaught, with many wounded and captured. Private Daniel Purdy age 21 (born June 10, 1842) of Company C, was struck in his left shoulder, the bullet passing into his lung. He was assisted by fellow comrades back through the town as the Union line retreated to Cemetery Hill.

Within the report of the New York Relief Agency we read of Private Purdy's last hours of earthy life. ". . . By the light of a candle held in a reversed bayonet, some of his fellow soldiers, and a clergyman and others gathered around his tent where he lay upon a bundle of hay. A prayer was offered up by the clergyman that the way of death might not be dark to him.

"When the prayer ceased, young Purdy astonished the group around him by quoting text upon text, the most beautiful of all the promises of the Christian religion; while repeating these, his ear caught the sound of a familiar hymn sung in a neighboring tent, and his face became radiant with devotion—death was not dark to him."[65]

Private Purdy stepped into eternal light the evening of July 15th.

There are two known Confederate soldiers buried in the Connecticut section. Both were probably placed within this plot because of the similarity of the state abbreviations on their wooden headboards. Both men were from the Carolinas.

Corporal David Williams
Company D, 20th North Carolina Infantry
Row B, #8

Corporal Williams was 25 years of age, 5 feet, 9 inches in height and listed his occupation as a farmer. He enlisted in the 20th North Carolina on June 25, 1861 and served as a cook until May 1862.

Corporal Williams was killed July 1st in the abortive and mismanaged attack of Brig. Gen. Iverson's Brigade against the Union line on Oak Ridge. The 20th North Carolina was near the left of the Brigade's line of march and received such destructive flanking fire that men were cut down in perfect rows.

Lieutenant Sidney Carter
Company A, 14th South Carolina Infantry
Row A, #5

While little is known of the individual lives of the Confederate soldiers buried in the Gettysburg National Cemetery, the exception is Lieutenant Sidney Carter. His many letters to his wife, through the commendable transcribing and genealogical research of Horace Fraser Rudisill of Darlington, South Carolina have been compiled in a book entitled "Dear Bet." The original letters, a gift from Bessie Mell Lane, are preserved in the Darlington Historical Society.

Sidney Carter was born in 1832 of Susan Ingram and Charles Powell Carter, the 9th child of a family of 12. (Charles Powell Carter, born March 6, 1797—died March 5, 1880; Susan Ingram Carter, born May 26, 1802—died September 18, 1862) The Carters were a distinguished family of Darlington County, tracing their roots back to 1767 when Sidney's great grandfather, Charles Powell Carter settled the area.

On October 16, 1855, Sidney then 23, married Ellen Timmons age 18 of Effingham, South Carolina. Ellen also came from a large and prominent family of the State. Her father, William Timmons, who had died in 1843, was a wealthy planter, while her uncle, Rev. John Morgan Timmons was a Baptist pastor and would be one of the signers of South Carolina's Ordinance of Secession in 1861. One of Ellen's older sisters, Caroline had married Sidney's older brother, William. Sidney and Ellen would have three children, Ida S. born in 1857, Horace W. born in 1859, and Minnie E. born 1861.

Even before the shots upon Fort Sumter were fired, the men of South Carolina were rallying to defend their State. Sidney and his elder brother William were already members of the local militia unit, the Lynches Creek Guards. This unit became Company A of the 14th South Carolina Infantry in August of 1861. Four of the six Carter brothers were mustered into the Regiment on August 10th; William age 28, James Morgan age 27, Sidney age 29, and Richard Daniel age 25. The oldest of the brothers, Giles age 40 would not join the regiment until March 17, 1862. The final brother, John age 36, enlisted in Company F, 1st South Carolina March 24, 1862. Of the six brothers, three would die during the war: Richard of disease on April 18, 1862, James at the battle of Chancellorsville May 3rd, 1863 and Sidney at Gettysburg, on July 8th. Giles was wounded at Gettysburg and taken as a prisoner of war to David Island Prison, New York City. He was exchanged September 16, 1863. William rose in rank to Major of the 14th South Carolina, but resigned due to poor health February 20, 1863. John served throughout the war.

The letters that Lieutenant Sidney Carter wrote to his wife, whom he fondly called "Bet," reveal the daily routine of a Civil War soldier, but also the daily stress of life on the Southern home front. In many of the letters Sidney wrote giving advice to Bet on the operation of the farm.

"You want to know what Hudson (the overseer on the farm) will do for nails. I can't say a word if he can't get them there. See if you can't get father or Will or Giles to get some salt. You must try yourself. If you can't find out where you can get some on credit. You will have to beg." (December 18, 1862)

"I have concluded it will be better to sell my cotton and you can find out what you can get for it. Try and get twenty cents for it, if possible—sell though, if you can't get but 18 cents of H. and C. . . . ." (March 15, 1863)

Of course he always spoke about the children in his letters.

". . . Ida has got her basket. She has had a gold dollar and I have procured two more for Horace and Minnie. tell them Papa sent them. If you will examine them you will see the marks for their names. Tell Ida she is big enough now to learn to spell. When I come home she must spell some for me." (January 15, 1862)

"Tell Ida and poor little Horace they don't want to see Papa any more than he wants to see them, but he don't cry much about it." (June 23, 1862)[66]

Imagine the heartache felt by all the children, North and South, separated from their ''papas'' for such a long time. In the spring of 1863, Ida and Horace became gravely ill.

"It would not be a shock to me to hear of the death of Horace or Ida, for I have heard of their sickness and have framed my mind to meet the worst. Tell them Pa has not forgotten them and fain would come to see them if he could. . . . Bet, there is a great consolation if they do (die) for sometimes I am almost tempted to wish that I had died when small like them. You must do the best you can and meet trouble like a soldier. I feel sad when I think how they are suffering in sickness—and you. How hard you will work to nurse them.'' (April 23, 1863)[67]

Thankfully both Ida and Horace recovered. Ida lived to 1926, Horace to 1912 and Minnie died in 1918. Seldom does Sidney speak of the possibility of his own death. He was slightly wounded at Gaines Mill on June 27, 1862.

"Bet, you must meet trouble halfway, for if I was not born to be killed by the Yankees, all the Yankees born can't hurt me. And if they kill me in battle remember I am fighting for God and country. When I think about being killed and leaving you and my dear little children it nerves me, for I feel like I am in the right and will come through safe and sound, and it makes me mad to look at them (Yankees) walking on the soil of South Carolina.'' (December 10, 1861)[68]

Later he wrote, ''Dear Bet, I begin to want to see this war close. Not that I want to give up to the Yankees, Never, but I want to see you all so bad.'' (September 1862)

With the summer of 1863 approaching, Confederate hopes of victory and the close of the war were at their peak. ''Bet, I sometimes think that this war is near its terminus.'' (April 26, 1863) The Confederate Army of Northern Virginia swept northward through the Shenandoah and Cumberland Valleys into the rich farmland of central Pennsylvania. Lieutenant Carter wrote of the hard marching in his last letter:

"We have had quite a hot time of it I assure you. . . . For myself, I had to leave ranks Thursday for the first time since I have been in service. I got over hot and liked to have fainted. I stopped in a shade and soon recovered and got in an ambulance and rode about a mile, where the army had stopped for the night. . . . It is generally believed we are going into enemy's land. If so I hope I may keep well and hearty so I won't have to leave ranks for the Yankees to get me over there.'' (June 21, 1863 written at Winchester, Virginia)[69]

The afternoon of July 1st, saw the 14th South Carolina hurled against the Union fortifications around the Lutheran Seminary buildings. ''Here the 14th Regiment was staggered for a moment by the severity and destructiveness of the enemy's musketry. It looked to us as though this regiment was entirely destroyed.''[70] The regiment suffered severely, but ''most gallantly stood its ground.'' The Union line was finally breached and driven back into the town.

Lieutenant Carter was struck down in this action, the bullet entering his chest and passing downward into his internal organs. The Carter's trusted slave, Dave, stayed by the mortally wounded Lieutenant until Friday evening, July 3rd when the Confederate army began their retreat back to Virginia. ''Dave said Sid told him to tell us to meet him in heaven, that he would never see us again. . . . and appeared to be praying all the time, tho so weak he could hardly be understood.'' Dave walked the several hundred miles back to Darlington, carrying the personal effects of his master to the grieving family. Along the way, Dave lost the watch which was to be given to little Horace. Lieutenant Sidney Carter died of his wounds on July 8th. His beloved wife Bet, died 14 years later, July 14, 1877.

The family accepted the supposition that their beloved brother, husband and father was laid in an unmarked and uncared for grave of Pennsylvania soil, never realizing that because of a minor mistake by the burial detail their beloved ''Sid'' would receive instead an honorable and sacred resting place. He rests here, testifying to the fact that our nation is no longer divided and that ''we are all Americans again this day.''

''. . . Kiss the dear little ones for me and accept all my love for yourself and them. I remain as ever your own. Sid.''[71]

Wisconsin Plot

A large number of the soldiers buried within the Wisconsin plot belonged to the framed Iron Brigade, recognized by their black Hardee hats. The Brigade suffered such high losses that it was only a shadow of its former strength after the battle. The regiments of the Iron Brigade (2nd, 6th, 7th, Wisconsin, 19th Indiana, and 24th Michigan) as well as all the units of the First Corps had effectively delayed the Confederate advance that 1st of July west of town, gaining the precious time needed for other Union forces to occupy the strong defensive positions south of the town.

Lieutenant Colonel George H. Stevens
2nd Wisconsin
Row D, #10

Here lies the second highest ranking Union officer buried in this Cemetery who was a casualty of the Gettysburg battle, Lieutenant Colonel George H. Stevens, age 31. He received his commission as Lieutenant Colonel on January 26, 1863. The highest ranking officer who was a casualty of Gettysburg buried in the Cemetery is located in the New York section, Lieutenant Colonel Max Thoman, commander of the 59th New York Regiment. (Lieutenant Colonel Thoman will be discussed later.) He was promoted to the rank of Lieutenant Colonel on January 8, 1863, only 18 days before Lieutenant Colonel Stevens.

As the First Corps advanced onto the battlefield west of the town the morning of July 1st, the 2nd Wisconsin was one of the first regiments to engage the enemy. As the regiment reached the crest of McPherson's Ridge it "received a volley of musketry from the enemy's line, from which many officers and men fell, among them Lieut. Colonel Stevens, mortally wounded."[35] Stevens died from his wound July 5th.

He left behind in Janesville, Wisconsin, his wife Harriet and two small children. George Stevens and Harriet were married at Fox Lake, Wisconsin the 28th day of March 1860. Their first child, Walter, was born February 10, 1860, while their 2nd child, Lucy was born July 15, 1861. Yes, the date of Walter's birth is correct a full month before his parents would be married. Harriet remarried in 1867.[72]

Lieut. Col. George H. Stevens, 2nd Wisconsin. (State Historical Society of Wisconsin)

Sergeant Walker S. Rouse
Company E, 2nd Wisconsin Infantry
Row D, #4

Walker Rouse was born July 4, 1840 in Litchfield, Connecticut. His parents, Elijah and Harriet Rouse journeyed westward, settling in Fon Du Lac, Wisconsin in the mid 1840s. At the age of 21, Walker enlisted in the 2nd Wisconsin, April 20, 1861, only a few days after the firing upon Fort Sumter.

In his first battle, First Bull Run July 31st, he was slightly wounded. Promoted to sergeant December 31st, he was wounded a second time at Groveton, Virginia August 28, 1862. At Gettysburg on July 1st, the 2nd Wisconsin stubbornly fought on McPherson's Ridge and it was here that

Company E, 2nd Wisconsin—Sergt. Walker Rouse is seated on the right. (USMHI)

Sergeant Rouse received his 3rd and this time fatal wound, a bullet in his left arm. He died on July 11th, only a few days after his 23rd birthday and the 87th birthday of the nation that he died to preserve.

Sergeant Albert E. Tarbox
Company K, 6th Wisconsin Infantry
Row D, #6

The stone over this grave reads "unknown," but research reveals that the soldier buried here is Sergeant Albert E. Tarbox. He enlisted in the 6th Wisconsin at the age of 19. His occupation before the war was that of a lumberman. He was 5 feet, 8 inches in height, with a dark complexion, black hair and piercing black eyes.

On the morning of July 1st, the 6th Wisconsin was detached from the Iron Brigade and held in reserve. Part of Brig. General Joseph Davis' Confederate Brigade had occupied a railroad cut north of the Chambersburg Pike. The commander of the 6th Wisconsin, Lieutenant Colonel Rufus Dawes led his regiment, with two New York regiments supporting his left, in a magnificent charge against this railroad cut. The Wisconsin line surged forward with "yells enough to almost awaken the dead."[73] The Regiment was soon on the brink of the cut, shouting for the Confederates massed below them to "throw down your muskets." The Union counter-charge had bagged almost 250 enemy prisoners.

Private James Sullivan of Company K was wounded in the left shoulder, "knocked me down as quick as if I had been hit with a sledge hammer. . . . Sergeant Tarbox came up the side of the cut and seeing me says, 'They've got you down Mickey, have they?' and then fell forward dead, (struck in the head) some of the damned rebs who had surrendered having shot him as he straightened up."[74]

Corporal John T. Christy
Company F, 2nd Wisconsin Infantry
Row B, #6

In the late afternoon of July 1st, the Union resistance on McPherson's Ridge had crumbled. Corporal John Christy from Racine County, Wisconsin, age 20, was wounded in the foot, and the Confederate advance passed over him. He was taken prisoner, but received limited medical treatment. When the Confederate army retreated July 5th, Christy was left behind. Federal doctors were forced to amputate his leg due to massive infection. His condition worsened, until he passed away on July 11th.

John's true name was Christensen. Why he enlisted in April of 1861 under an alias is a mystery. His mother, Hannah, was still alive, living in Waterford, Wisconsin, while his father, Andreas Christensen had died in 1847. John had been born in Copenhagen, Denmark and brought to America as a baby.

Private James Perrine
Company I, 2nd Wisconsin Infantry
Row C, #18

Resting in this grave is a young man who should not have died, but through someone's incompetence, his life was taken from him.

Private Perrine was 27 when he enlisted in Company I of the 2nd Wisconsin on June 11th, 1861, from Dodgeville, Wisconsin. Ironically he served as an assistant nurse for five months. At Gettysburg he received a wound to his arm that was not mortal. After a month recuperating in the general hospital, his arm was sufficiently healed so that he was eagerly looking forward to going home on a furlough.

Opium pills and morphine were widely given to ease the pain of the patients. Sophronia E. Bucklin, a volunteer nurse with the U.S. Sanitary Commission recorded what she saw the morning of August 19th when Private Perrine took his daily pain medicine.

"... He was seized with a deadly coldness, and shivered incessantly, his muscles contracted with jerking movement, and great sweat-drops gathered on his cold forehead. ... the surgeon was summoned, but he could do nothing to break the chill of death, which was slowly stealing over him. He reached for my hand, and retained it, till one by one his senses left him. Just before the last convulsive shiver ran through his veins, one of the attendants took it from his grasp, remarking that it was a bad sign for any one to hold the hand of another when death came to the heart.

"He was then too far gone to realize anything, and at eleven o'clock he died. The last prescription by some awful mistake was deadly poison and nothing could have saved him."[75]

Cpl. John T. Christy, 2nd Wisconsin. (State Historical Society of Wisconsin)

New Jersey Plot

Within the New Jersey plot are several stones with only initials carved upon them. Most of these men can now be identified, such as Martin Van Houten (Row C, #19), James Flavigar (Row C, #6), and Henry Rourke (Row B, #21)

Private George W. Adams
Company F, 12th New Jersey Infantry
Row A, #14

In his book, "The Struggle for the Bliss Farm at Gettysburg," historian Elwood Christ accounts the early morning attack upon the Bliss buildings by the 12th New Jersey.

"About 8:00 a.m. Capt. Thompson led his men up to the Brian barn, down the farm lane, and across the Emmitsburg Road to a point a short distance to the west. There the Jerseymen formed into columns by companies, using the crest of the broad, flat knoll as partial cover. As soon as they were in formation, with company F in the van, the detachment charged the barn."[76]

As the five New Jersey companies swept up over the crest of that flat knoll, they received a hailstorm of bullets and artillery fire from the Confederate line, several men of Company F being struck down. One was Private George Adams, hit by a shell fragment in his thigh.

Private Adams was from Beverly, New Jersey of Gloucester County. When he enlisted on August 9, 1862, he was only 19 years of age, born March 18, 1843. He was described as "a boy of quiet disposition who seemed to be old—much beyond his years, and not desirous of making many friends, or of participating in our sports or conversations; but minded his own business and attended strictly to duties, whilst his bravery was unquestioned."[77]

Private William A. Ezekiel
Company I, 7th New Jersey Infantry
Row C, #1

William Ezekiel and Susan Cole were married July 3rd, 1858. Five years later, less a day, William would be killed in a Peach Orchard on the battlefield of Gettysburg. They lived in Beemerville, New Jersey and would see three children born in their brief life together: twins, Edgar and Phebe, born May 7, 1859, and William born January 31, 1862. Susan was devoted to the memory of her husband, dying December 1906, having never remarried.

Priv. Simon Creamer, Co. K, 12th New Jersey Infantry—buried in Row A, grave #20, New Jersey section. Priv. Creamer had been attached to Battery A, 1st Rhode Island since April 30, 1863. He died instantly when an enemy shell decapitated him on July 3rd.
(Last Full Measure, John Busey)

Private Joseph Hall
Company F, 7th New Jersey Infantry
Row B, #20

Many men enlisted with great expectations of glory, only to experience filthy living conditions, hunger, exposure, boredom and sickness. Joseph Hall enlisted in the 7th New Jersey at Trenton, September 2, 1861. In the winter of 1862–63 in an army hospital suffering from illness, he resolved to go home and therefore deserted. He eluded the military patrols for about a week, before being arrested in northern Virginia, on February 3rd. The military court was lenient in their punishment, only deducting $8.30 from his service pay to cover the cost of his "arrest and transportation" back to his regiment.

During the Gettysburg battle, the Union Third Corps was advanced to an exposed position along the Emmitsburg Road, the apex of the line being at the Peach Orchard. The Confederate Brigades of Generals Barksdale, Wofford, and Kershaw broke that apex and swept the Union defenders back toward Cemetery Ridge. The 7th New Jersey was shifted to assist the Union defense in the Orchard, but was caught up in the current of retreat. Private Hall was killed in this action. He left in Patterson, New Jersey his wife of 12 years, Bridget, and two daughters, Elizabeth age 9, and Sarah who had just celebrated her 10th birthday the day before her father was killed.

Private James Bennett
Company F, 7th New Jersey Infantry
Row B, #19

James Bennett was also killed in the fighting near the famous Peach Orchard, July 2nd. Research into his life raised many questions. What is known is that he was age 36 when he enlisted, September 2, 1861, being 5 feet, 6 ¾ inches in height, dark complexion and hair, with hazel colored eyes. He listed his occupation as a farmer and laborer. He had been born in Weath, Ireland, and it is here where the questions arise. The records reveal that his parents, Matthew and Catharine Bennett were married in Ireland July 20, 1803. Matthew died March 10, 1831 after coming to America. Their son never married, choosing to stay at home to care for his mother. The unusual element of this story is that when James was killed at Gettysburg his mother was 90 years of age, and thus would have been near 52 in 1825 when James was born. All the evidence, even the last letter James wrote to her on June 2nd, points to the fact that she was his natural mother. Having a child at the age of 52 is not impossible, but it is certainly remarkable.[78]

Pennsylvania Plot

Major General Charles Collis

The Pennsylvania plot is dominated by the special grave memorial of Major General Charles Collis. It is a high backed bench surmounted with a bust of the general. General Collis is gazing westward toward Seminary Ridge and his country estate. He constructed this home in 1900 and named it "Red Patch," in honor of the red diamond patch worn by the soldiers of his command: the 114th Pennsylvania Regiment.

Charles Collis was born within a wealthy family of Ireland, February 4, 1838. At the age of 15 he and his father traveled to America, settling in Philadelphia. After a few weeks, his mother, five sisters, and two brothers also sailed for America, aboard the "City of Glasgow." The ship never reached American shores, sinking in the Atlantic with no survivors.

Collis studied law under Mr. John M. Read (who would become Chief Justice of the Pennsylvania Supreme Court), passing the bar in 1859. When the war began, he enlisted for three months in the 18th Pennsylvania Regiment as Sergeant Major. Upon the termination of the regiment's service, Collis was given permission to organize a company and then a full regiment, the 114th Pennsylvania, which was commonly called "Collis' Zouaves."

Major General Charles H.T. Collis

The grave of Major General Charles H.T. Collis.

51

On the battlefield of Fredericksburg, December 13th, 1862, Colonel Collis' leadership would merit the receiving of the Medal of Honor. The Brigade in which the 114th Pennsylvania was attached "was brought into action at the critical moment" when other Union units were retiring. "The enemy's infantry were pursuing the reserves, while the rebel batteries on the ridge were keeping up a terrible fire of solid shot and shell." Two Union batteries were on the verge of being captured, when the Brigade (Robinson's), came rushing onto the field. "Gen. Robinson's horse was disemboweled by a solid shot: his adjutant-general was severely wounded, and his bugler killed, while they were all riding at the head of the column." Lying on the ground General Robinson called out to Colonel Collis; "Pitch in, pitch in Colonel." Collis "quickly took in the situation and seizing the colors of his regiment from the color-sergeant, galloped with them to the front, deploying his regiment into line of battle at the same time, and attacking the advancing foe with the bayonet. The charge of the Zouaves was not only brilliant, but picturesque, as they were uniformed in scarlet and blue, their heads being decorated with the red fez and white turban of the French Zouaves d'Afrique."[79]

Because of illness, Colonel Collis did not lead the 114th Pennsylvania at Gettysburg. Afterwards he was breveted to the rank of Brigadier General and in the 1864 campaign commanded an independent brigade of one cavalry and six infantry regiments, detached for special duty at the head-quarters of General U.S. Grant. In the fighting at Fort Sedgwick outside Petersburg, Virginia, he led the assaulting column and displayed such bravery that he was breveted Major General on the battlefield.

After the war, Collis returned to Philadelphia to practice law and become involved in local politics. He served as Assistant City Solicitor and in 1869 was appointed Director of the City Trust. In 1871 he was elected as City Solicitor and re-elected in 1874. His political career took him to New York City where he was involved in many public works, especially the paving of the city's streets.

General Collis had married Septima M. Levy of Charleston, South Carolina on December 9, 1861. They had three children. On May 10, 1902, General Collis took severely ill at his Gettysburg home and was rushed to Bryn Mawr Hospital outside Philadelphia, where he died the next day, his three children by his side. His wife was at that time traveling in Russia. General Collis requested that he be buried here, close to the graves of his fallen comrades, whom he had been unable to lead in the Gettysburg battle. His wife is not buried here; she died in 1917 in France.[80]

Unknown Zouaves
Row F, #6–12

These graves are marked as "unknown Zouaves," members of the 114th Pennsylvania, "Collis Zouaves." The name Zouave always brings up the question—what are

Two members of the 114th Pa. (Collis Zouaves) (Division of Archives & Manuscripts Pa. Historical & Museum Commission)

they? Before the war there was an avid interest in our sister Republic, France, particularly that which pertained to the military. Napoleon had revolutionized warfare, the Marquis de Lafayette was beloved in our country, and the French Foreign Legion had been formed in 1831. In North Africa part of the Legion had adopted a distinctive uniform composed of balloon pantaloons, a short open jacket, gaiters on the legs and topped by a turban or fez. These uniforms were also of bright colors. These French units adopted the Moroccan tribal name of "Zouave." American militia units were attracted to the fancy uniforms and the precision drill of the French Zouaves and thus copied them even to the use of the name, "Zouave." At the beginning of the Civil War, many of these American Zouave militia units enlisted in the organized armies of both the Union and Confederacy, still wearing their colorful and distinctive uniforms. Needless to say, in the early battles, confusion reigned due in part to the many different un-uniformed units. By 1863 most of the Zouave regiments had discarded their bright garb, but still retained the Zouave name.

The Pennsylvania Zouaves buried here, died at the Sherfy Farm, near the famous Peach Orchard on July 2nd. The men in graves #9, #10, #11, are recorded to have been burnt to death when the Sherfy barn was accidently consumed in flames. These men, being wounded, could not escape the fire, and suffered a most horrible death.

Corporal Nathan B. Wilcox
Company A, 149th Pennsylvania Infantry
Row A, #12

The last name of this soldier was not known when the grave stone was carved, but by researching the regimental roster of the 149th Pennsylvania, we can determine that here rests Corporal Nathan Wilcox. Corporal Wilcox was from Wellsboro, Pennsylvania, enlisting in the regiment August 8, 1862 at age 19. He was the eldest of a family of seven children. His father, Daniel Wilcox had died in 1855 leaving Nathan's mother, Abigail to care for the large family. Nathan therefore probably enlisted for the sole purpose of providing more money for his mother and family. He was killed instantly by a shell during the fierce fighting around the McPherson's barn, July 1st.

Cpl. Nathan B. Wilcox 149th Pa. (USMHI)

Private Stephen Kelly
Company E, 91st Pennsylvania Infantry
Row A, #88

The stone marking this grave reads "unknown," but when originally carved in 1864, it read, "Stephen Kelly."

Kelly had enlisted in the 91st Pennsylvania August 21, 1861 at Philadelphia, 27 years of age. During the 2nd battle of Fredericksburg, May 3rd, 1863, he was captured and held as a prisoner for two weeks until exchanged. During the Gettysburg Campaign, Private Kelly took sick and was taken to a hospital in Baltimore. His regiment fought on the summit of Little Round Top, but Private Kelly missed the battle. He served through the remainder of the war and was mustered out of the service July 10, 1865, near Washington. After the war he lived in Philadelphia.

Every year thousands of visitors travel to Gettysburg on vacation. In the years after the Civil War, likewise thousands of visitors traveled to the battlefield. Many were veterans searching for those battlefield sites where they had stood in combat, facing death, and beating the grim reaper. Many also strolled through the National Cemetery searching for the graves of their fallen comrades who had not beaten the foe of death. Imagine the shock and the surprise of Stephen Kelly as he searched the Pennsylvania section for fallen comrades' graves and lo found his own name on this grave marker. He of course wasn't dead. The stone was therefore changed to read "unknown."

The reason why the burial detail mistook the unknown soldier to be Stephen Kelly is easy to explain. Shortly before the Gettysburg battle, when Kelly became ill, his knapsack with his name and regimental number stenciled upon it, was stolen by an unknown thief. This unknown thief was killed during the battle wearing Kelly's knapsack and is therefore buried in this unknown grave.

The real Stephen Kelly died in 1889 and is buried in the Philadelphia National Cemetery.[81]

Private William Beaumont
Company A, 88th Pennsylvania Infantry
Row B, #73

Resting in this grave is one of the three Beaumont brothers who served during the Civil War in the 88th Pennsylvania Regiment. It was a common practice during the war for family members, fathers, sons, brothers, cousins to serve in the same units. This policy was ended after the Second World War due to the death of the five Sullivan brothers when the USS Juneau was sunk.

The three brothers, William age 23, George age 27, and John age 19 at the time of their enlistment in Company A of the 88th on August 23, 1861 were from St. Clair, Pennsylvania. All three had worked in the anthracite coal mines of Schuylkill County.

The 88th Pennsylvania was positioned on Oak Ridge behind a stone wall where it assisted in repelling the attack of Iverson's North Carolina Brigade. During this action William was struck in the neck by a bullet. He died 12 days later, July 13th and rests in this grave. In the late afternoon retreat of the Union First Corps through the streets of Gettysburg, younger brother John was captured. He was held as a prisoner until July 21st when paroled at City Point, Virginia. He would be killed nearly a year later in the fortifications of Petersburg on June 18, 1864.

The eldest brother, George, survived the war, though he was wounded in his left wrist at Gettysburg and would have his left thumb shot off at Laurel Hill, Virginia May 8, 1864. After the war he returned to labor in the subterranean darkness of the St. Clair coal mines. He was killed in the mine on November 30th, 1868 when he was struck in the head by a falling chunk of coal.[82]

Private Charles Frederick Gardner
Company H, 110th Pennsylvania Infantry
Row C, #14

Colonel St. Clair Mulholland commander of the 116th Pennsylvania Regiment, led his men past the already bloody Wheatfield the afternoon of July 2nd. His regiment took position on a small rocky hillock. Colonel Mulholland relates:

"In front and a little to the right stood the Rose Farm house and barn. Over the little valley in the immediate front one could see the enemy massed and preparing for another attack. The dead of the One Hundred and Tenth Pennsylvania Volunteers lay directly in front, on the ground which that command had vacated but a half hour before, and one young boy lay outstretched on a large rock with his musket still grasped in his hand, his pale calm face upturned to the sunny sky, the warm blood still flowing from a hold in his forehead and running in a red stream over the gray stone. The young hero had just given his life for his country. A sweet, childish face it was, lips parted in a smile—those still lips on which the mother's kisses had so lately fallen, warm and tender. The writer never looked on a soldier slain without feeling that he gazed upon the relics of a saint; but the little boy lying there with his blood coloring the soil of his own state, and his young heart stilled forever, seemed more like an angel form than any of the others."[83]

This young soldier whose death had so touched Colonel Mulholland's emotions was Private Charles F. Gardner. He was born in England, 1843, the second son of Henry and Harriet Elizabeth Gardner. He had 3 brothers and 2 sisters.

The family had immigrated to America in the late 1850s, shortly after the death of Charles' mother in England, December 28, 1856. Colonel Mulholland's thoughts of "those still lips" were incorrect in regards to his "mother's kisses," but surely when young Charles marched off to war in September of 1862, his two younger sisters showered him with loving good-by kisses.

On June 18, 1863, Charles penned his last letter to his father; "It is with the greatest of pleasure I write you a few lines to let you know how I am getting along and where I am." He then speaks of the hard marching since leaving Fredericksburg; 14 miles the first day, then 12, followed by 33, 25, 10 and 22 miles each day thereafter. "We have been laying here (Centerville) since yesterday afternoon. The weather is still very hot. We have got good news here now that the Rebels are in Penn. . . . It just what we want, it will be the means of bringing the war to a close some sooner I think." He closed his letter, "Yours until death." That prophecy came to pass only two weeks later, on the edge of a Wheatfield that became hollowed ground with the mingled blood of thousands.[84]

Cpl. Joseph S. Gutelius, Co. D, 150th Pennsylvania, buried in Row A, grave #11 of the Pa. section. During the retreat of July 1st, Cpl. Gutelius, though wounded, carried the state colors of the regiment. At the corner of S. Washington and High Street he sat down on a doorstep to rest being exhausted. However a small company of North Carolina soldiers rounded the corner and sighted the flag. "A rattle of musketry was heard, and the brave corporal fell dead with the flag clasped in his hands." The flag was seized by Lieut. F.M. Harney of the 14th N.C. Shortly after this incident, Lieut. Harney was himself mortally wounded. His dying request was that the captured Pennsylvania flag be presented to the President of the Confederacy, Jefferson Davis. At the war's end, April 1865, when Pres. Davis was captured by Union forces, this same flag carried by Cpl. Gutelius was discovered in Davis' personal baggage. (Advance the Colors)

Private Amos P. Sweet
Company H, 150th Pennsylvania Infantry
Row C, #37

Amos Sweet and Atlanta Fanner were married on March 18, 1860 in Crawford County, Pennsylvania. They were both in their early twenties. Two and a half years later they were blessed with the birth of their only child, Amy, born on August 20, 1862. Ten days after Amy's birth, Amos was mustered into Company H of the 150th Pennsylvania Regiment.

Major General Abner Doubleday, temporary commander of the First Corps at Gettysburg on July 1st, wrote in his official report, that he "relied greatly" upon the three Pennsylvania regiments of the Bucktail Brigade, (143rd, 149th, 150th) "to hold the point assigned them," which was along the Chambersburg Pike at the McPherson farm. "My confidence in this noble body of men was not misplaced . . . they repulsed the repeated attacks of vastly superior numbers at close quarters and maintained their position until the final retreat of the whole line."[29] Out of 400 engaged of the 150th, the regiment suffered a loss of 66%. Private Sweet was wounded in his right leg. He was carried into the town where his leg was amputated in the Saint Francis Xavier Catholic Church located on West High Street.

After the amputation, he along with several others were beded in the house of Peter Myers a few doors from the Catholic Church. Mr. Myers' oldest daughter, Elizabeth "Sallie" Myers was a school teacher in Gettysburg. She spoke of her experience and the death of Private Sweet.

"He had been with us several days and had become very fond of my little sisters (Susan) very frequently they sang for him. His favorite was "There is No Name So Sweet on Earth,' at that time a popular Sunday School hymn. He suffered from indigestion, and one night in his restlessness, the bandages became loose. It was after midnight, the nurse tired out, had fallen asleep and before we could find a surgeon he was so weakened by loss of blood that he died the next morning." (July 15th)

Sallie mentioned that his last words were, "tell my wife I am going home." Atlanta Sweet, upon hearing of her husband's wounding rushed to Gettysburg, but unfortunately arrived several days after his death. "Her grief was heartrending."[85]

2nd Lieutenant William H. Smith
Company B, 106th Pennsylvania Infantry
Row C, #42

The late afternoon of July 2nd, companies A & B of the 106th Pennsylvania were on skirmish duty near the Codori Farm, beyond the Emmitsburg Road, while about 400 yards northwest Confederates had re-occupied the Bliss Farm buildings. Company B, led by Captain James Lynch, was ordered to clean the "Rebs" out of the buildings. Ap-

proaching the barn they were challenged and received a volley. The firing from the barn continued, driving the Pennsylvanians back. Twelve men of the company were killed or wounded in this brief but fierce action, including 2nd Lieutenant William H. Smith.

Lieutenant Smith enlisted in the regiment August 1, 1861 at Philadelphia—though his home was Cape May, New Jersey. In the spring of 1863 he took a furlough and was united in marriage with Hannah Little on April 1st. They had a brief honeymoon before William was again on the front line leading his company and receiving his mortal wound. On December 28, 1863, Hannah gave birth to a son, whom she named William H. Smith Jr. in honor of the father that the little boy would only know by a photograph and the memories that his mother would share.

2nd Lieut. William H. Smith, 106th Pa. (USMHI)

2nd Lieutenant William H. Beaver
Company D, 153rd Pennsylvania Infantry
Row C, #80

The term of service of the 153rd Pennsylvania was soon to expire, but due to the extreme emergency of the Confederate invasion, it joined the ranks of the Army of the Potomac in its march to Gettysburg. It was now Pennsylvania, their native soil which was threatened by the "Rebels." The 153rd was attached to the Brigade of Colonel Leopold Von Gilsa, of the XI Corps. This Union Corps was composed of many German and Eastern European immigrants and has through the years been unjustly maligned. On the afternoon of July 1st it was routed from the fields north of Gettsyburg back through the town, but not before it had savagely resisted the Confederate assault from front and flank. The 153rd Pennsylvania was on the right flank of the Corps at Barlow's Knoll and bore much of the Confederate attack, losing over 200 men out of a strength of 497, a loss of 43%.

Lieutenant Beaver of East Allen, Pennsylvania led Company D of the regiment. The fighting surged around the hillock, where Lieutenant Beaver fell with a mortal wound. He died shortly afterwards at the Almshouse, being only 21 years of age.

2nd Lieut. William H. Beaver, 153rd Pa. (153rd Pa. Regimental)

Confederate Soldiers
Private James Akers
Company K, 2nd Mississippi Infantry
Row D, #26

It's a perplexing mystery in regards to how this Mississippi soldier was mistakenly buried here. With the other Confederate burials, the similarity of their state abbreviations with those of the state plots they are buried in seems the most plausible explanation. However this individual served from a state whose abbreviation doesn't come close to resembling that of Pennsylvania. Could he have been wearing some part of a Union uniform? He was killed July 3rd during the grand charge against the Union center on Cemetery Ridge. Therefore was he buried by fellow comrades or by a Union burial detail? The questions are many, but the fact remains, he is buried here.

James Akers was only 17 when he enlisted in the 2nd Mississippi on July 1, 1862. He is one of the youngest soldiers buried within the National Cemetery. The Confederate Congress had passed a conscription act on April 16, 1862, drafting into service all males between 18 and 35. James' older brother John was summoned to report for duty. Both the Federal and Confederate governments allowed the practice of substitutes for those who desired not to serve. For some reason, perhaps his family, or economic responsibilities on the plantation, John choose not to serve. He accepted his younger brother, James to be his substitute in the Confederate army. You will notice on the headstone, that James Akers is buried under his brother's name, John.

James Akers' military service file, records that he was of average height, 5 feet, 6 inches, a fair complexion, with auburn hair and blue eyes. He was a student at Iuka, Mississippi.

Confederate Secretary of War, George W. Randolph wrote on August 12, 1862: "I think that medals conferred as rewards for good conduct in the field cultivate the spirit which distinguishes the patriot soldier from the mercenary." This recommendation by the secretary to award medals to Confederate soldiers was authorized by the Confederate Congress on October 13, 1862. However no Confederate "Medals of Honor" were ever awarded nor even made, due to the fact that the money allocated was stolen by an individual posing as an agent to buy the needed machinery and seals in England. The Richmond government urged all units in the Confederate service to supply names of soldiers who had performed acts of heroism to a "Roll of Honor" in the expectation that Medals of Honor would be awarded to these men after the war. Private James Akers' name appears on this Confederate "Roll of Honor" for valor displayed in the battle of Gettysburg.[86]

Sergeant Thomas J. Graves
Company I, 21st Georgia Infantry
Row D, #30

Private Graves enlisted in the 21st Georgia from Stewart County on July 17, 1861. He was 32 years of age when he enlisted. During the 2nd day of battle there was incessant skirmishing between the lines. Private Graves, whose unit was positioned on the western outskirts of the town received a mortal wound in this skirmishing. He was carried into the Union lines to a hospital in the rear. He died on September 3rd.

Private Greshem G. Williams
Company A, 3rd Georgia Infantry
Row E, #49

Private Williams was mortally wounded in the early evening of July 2nd, as the 3rd Georgia of Brig. General Wright's Brigade was attacking across the Codori Farm against Cemetery Ridge. Private Williams was captured along with a large number of the 3rd and 48th Georgia by the 106th Pennsylvania in the barnyard. He died a few days later on July 9th. He was from Waynesboro, Georgia.

Private Eli T. Green
Company E, 14th Virginia Infantry
Row D, #61

Eli Green enlisted in the 14th Virginia May 12, 1861 at the age of 22. His home was Macklenburg, Virginia. The 14th Virginia was a part of Brig. General Lewis Armistead's Brigade of Major General Pickett's Division, which on July 3rd assaulted the Union center. General Armistead was mortally wounded while leading the final charge over the stone wall into the Angle. The flag of the 14th Virginia was carried over the wall alongside the gallant general. We do not know if Private Green was with the general and the flag as they surged over the wall, reaching the ''High Water Mark of the Confederacy,'' but it is possible. Private Green was struck two times: a bullet in his right hip, and another bullet which shattered his right arm below the elbow. He was carried to the rear, where his arm was amputated at the shoulder. He died at the General Hospital on August 15th.

Sergeant Isaac S. Osborne
Company I, 62nd Pennsylvania Infantry
Row D, #82

The storm of bullets seemed always to rage more intensely around the color guard of a regiment. The torn and tattered banners preserved in museums vividly testify to the courage displayed by those men whose duty it was to keep the colors up. Color Sergeant Isaac Osborne was one of such courage. He was killed the 2nd day of the battle in the furious fighting of the Wheatfield defending the colors.

He was born in 1831, one of five boys and five girls of Joseph and Kinter Osborne of Jefferson County, Pennsylvania. Isaac married Marie Aaron probably in 1850. They had one son, Jerome Bernard Osborne born November 13, 1851. Marie died six years later in 1857. The following year Isaac remarried, Mary Jane Baughman at Packer, Pennsylvania (May 13, 1858) and made their home in Shannondale. Two boys were born to the family, John (possibly in 1859) and Isaac who was born after his father's death at Gettysburg.

Sergeant Osborne on July 13, 1862 wrote this touching letter of fatherly advice to his eldest son, Jerome:

''I well know you are young yet to know the duty a son ot (ought) to have toward his father, but neveraless (sic) you are old a nuff (enough) to know from the learning that you have already got, that you ot (ought) to respect your father and write a letter every week or so. Know you my son if I an far away from you that I love you and your little brother John just as much as if I was with you, but God only knows weather (sic) I will every (sic) see either of your faces again in this world. But my dear children I want you to be good boys and as you Jerome is the oldest to be good and kind to all and go to Church as often as you can and take your little

Sergt. Isaac Osborne, (right) 62nd Pa. (courtesy of the family)

57

brother with you and learn him to love God and then if it is the will of God that your father don't live to return home to you—if you be good boys the same God that taked (took) your father from you will bless you and you both will be grate (great) men in this world and when you die the same God will take you to his bosom where you will be happy for every (sic)—and your kind father will pray for your good welfare as long as he lives to do so. I have been in many dangers since I left you but I put my hold (whole) trust in God and he has spared my life while a grate (great) many brave men was killed by my side and I was spared. But there are another grate (great) battle to be fought in a few days again and your father will be in it without any doubt, and the will of God be done—and if your father falls it will be at the head of his brave company and for the Union and the peace of our Country. My dear children I will to a close by asking you to always be true to your Country as your father has and every (sic) will be.

"And I pray God will bless my two sons and guide them through this world and at their death take them to Heaven where troubles will end."[87]

Isaac's widow would remarry in 1869 and live in Illinois, while the two younger boys John and Isaac would grow up and live in Illinois and San Francisco, California. (Isaac possibly died during the great San Francisco earthquake of 1906.)

After his father's death, the eldest son Jerome was "bounded" to his uncle, Jake Aaron, who labored the boy in the lumber business of western Pennsylvania. At the age of 17 Jerome ran away and for several years worked at many different jobs. After meeting her at a dance, he married Sarah Agnes Clark on September 15, 1874 in Brookville, Pennsylvania. Jerome became successful in the construction business, erecting many churches such as St. Joseph's in New Kensington, Pennsylvania, and successful as a father, raising 12 children. He died in 1948 at the grand age of 96. His father, Sergeant Isaac Osborne would have been proud.

Three soldiers of Company K

Near 7:30 p.m. July 2nd the Union line in the Peach Orchard and along the Emmitsburg Road had collapsed.

The Confederate tide surged through the Wheatfield, and into Plum Run Valley to the base of Little Round Top. In the gathering darkness the Pennsylvania Reserves of Major General Samuel Crawford counter-attacked off the slopes of the hill and hurled the Confederate tide back. The Pennsylvania Reserves stopped their charge at the edge of the Wheatfield which was by then littered with thousands of prostrate mangled bodies.

Company K of the 30th Pennsylvania was unique at Gettysburg; the entire company, 53 men, were composed of Gettysburg and Adams County men. This company has been termed as "the boys who fought at home." There are three members of Company K buried in the Pennsylvania section, of which only one was a casualty of the battle.

Private William McGrew
Company K, 30th Pennsylvania Infantry
Row F, #14

Private McGrew was wounded in the regiment's counter-attack the evening of July 2nd. He died in his own home in Mummasburg, just west of Gettysburg, August 26th, with his mother Jane McGrew by his side. He was age 23 and had been a shoemaker before the war.[88]

Private John W. McKinney
Company K, 30th Pennsylvania Infantry
Row E, #31

Private McKinney was already dead when the Gettysburg battle occurred. He had contracted Typhoid Fever and had died in the army hospital in Alexandria, Virginia February 24th, 1863. His mother, Eliza McKinney had her son's

Company K, 30th Pa. "The Boys who fought at home". (LC)

body transferred to the newly dedicated Gettysburg Cemetery.

The McKinneys were a typical farming family of the Gettysburg area with six children. John was the oldest of the family at the age of 20 when he died. The next brother, Robert Jr. was also a member of Company K and survived the war. The third son of the family, Andrew enlisted in another local unit, the 21st Pennsylvania Cavalry at the young age of 14. He died the next year, July 17, 1864 of disease at City Point, Virginia.

Private Elijah L. Leech
Company K, 30th Pennsylvania Infantry
Row G, #25

Private Leech is the third member of Company K buried in the Pennsylvania plot. He survived the carnage of Gettysburg and the war, being mustered out June 28, 1865. He married Elizabeth Molison on August 2, 1866 in the Methodist Church in Gettysburg. He died April 15, 1895. His wife, Elizabeth who died March 15, 1923 is buried here beside her husband.[89]

Private John McNutt
Company G, 140th Pennsylvania Infantry
Row F, #25

Private John McNutt was the oldest child, age 17 of William and Nancy McNutt, (married January 16, 1845) of Cannonsburg, Washington County, Pennsylvania. He had three brothers and four sisters. Private McNutt was killed July 2nd between the Peach Orchard and the Wheatfield on a small knoll called the "Stony Hill," overlooking the Rose Farm. His regiment, the right flank of Brig. General Zook's Brigade, sustained a loss of 47%.[90]

Private Frederick Reitinger
Company I, 87th Pennsylvania Infantry
Row G, #20

Frederick Reitinger did not fight in the battle of Gettysburg, but did serve in the campaign. When the Confederate army invaded Pennsylvania June 1863, it marched northward through the Shenandoah Valley capturing a Union garrison at Winchester, Virginia. During that engagement Reitinger suffered a rupture to his right side as he attempted to leap across a ditch. He was hospitalized at York, Pennsylvania and was transferred to the Invalid Corps. His service records tell us that he was married in 1857 to Sarah Fleming in Adams County. He enlisted in the 87th Pennsylvania in 1861 at the age of 24. He was 5 feet, 5 inches tall, with dark hair and complexion. After the war, he returned to Adams County, living near Hanover, 16 miles

southeast of Gettysburg. He died May 6, 1890. Sarah died in 1907 and was buried here with her husband. She was the first woman buried in the Gettysburg National Cemetery.

There are three other women resting in the semicircular burial site; Hannah S.J. Flaharty (1929) wife of Thomas Flaharty, 21st Pennsylvania Cavalry, (Row G, #45), Elizabeth Leech (1923) wife of Elijah Leech, (Row G, #24), and Annie M. Tinsley (1931) wife of William Tinsley, 5th Pennsylvania Cavalry (Row G, #31).

Priv. John McNutt, 140th Pa. (USMHI)

Vermont Plot

Private Benjamin N. Wright
Company I, 13th Vermont Infantry
Row B, #9

Gettysburg was the only full-scale engagement the 13th Vermont Regiment participated in during the war. It had been organized the summer of 1862, but had spent most of its service in the Washington, D.C. area, picketing and guarding military posts. Even though Gettysburg would be the regiment's baptism of fire the unit as well as the entire Vermont Brigade, would perform heroically. The regiment made a forced march to Gettysburg and in the late afternoon of July 2nd assisted in the repulse of the Confederate attack which had broken the advanced line of the Third Corps. In their counter-attack, the 13th Vermont advanced to the Roger's House along the Emmitsburg Road, where Private Benjamin Wright received a fatal wound in his breast and three lesser wounds.

On April 30, 1860 he had married Julia A. Payne, making their home in Washington County, Vermont. Benjamin died July 12th, and Julia never remarried, dying March 8, 1910.

Priv. Benjamin N. Wright, 13th Vermont. (13th Vermont Regimental)

Private Joseph Ashley
Company C, 16th Vermont Infantry
Row A, #2

Private Ashley is one of several former Canadians that are buried within the National Cemetery. He was born in Quebec of French Canadian parents in 1827. He lived in Canada until shortly after his marriage in 1859, moving to the town of Cavendish, near Hinesburg, Vermont. His wife, Phebe Geollett, was only 15 years of age when they were married. They had one child, a boy born in 1861, who they named Lewis. Tragically their beloved little boy only lived for three months, dying on December 3, 1861.

On August 17, 1862, Ashley enlisted in the 16th Vermont, which was only a nine months regiment. On July 3rd, possibly during the artillery bombardment preceding "Pickett's Charge," Private Ashley was killed by a shell fragment.[91]

Private William O. Doubleday
Company H, 14th Vermont Infantry
Row A, #19

While caring for the many wounded in the Catholic Church on West High Street, Mr. George H. Stuart of the U.S. Christian Commission paused to talk with Private Doubleday. A member of the 14th Vermont, Private Doubleday was 41 years of age from Sherburne, Vermont. His left leg was fractured during the fighting of July 3rd, and had been amputated. Mr. Stuart related their conversation:

> "When I enlisted (summer of 1862), which I did because I considered it a disgrace to be drafted, just as I was leaving for the war, my wife (Emma, they were married November 26, 1846) said, 'I hope you will come back all right and a good Christian.' It touched my heart. We went into the room with the family, and there she prayed for me, and then asked me to pray. I tried to offer a few broken petitions. My little boy, only thirteen years old, (either William born February 12, 1848 or Charles born November 5, 1849) then offered a most earnest prayer for me and for our distressed country. I don't know where he learned to pray like that, unless it was in the Sabbath School."[92]

Mr. Stuart witnessed tenderly to Private Doubleday of the love of God and his personal need of salvation through the risen Lord Jesus, "he pressed my hands, and the tears came fast as rain. I prayed with him . . . " Emma Doubleday arrived at her husband's side shortly before his death on August 12th. She expressed in a letter to Mr. Stuart "how her husband's peaceful death had answered her prayers."

William and Emma Doubleday had 5 sons, William, Charles, Otto born July 14, 1852, George born September 27, 1854, and Fred born November 15, 1860. Emma Doubleday was reunited in heaven with her husband on October 27, 1907.

Priv. Andrew E. Osgood, 13th Vermont. (13th Vermont Regimental)

Before the war, Andrew lived with his parents, George and Ann Osgood, and two younger brothers, on their rocky thin-soiled Vermont farm. The death of her son seemed too heavy a weight upon Ann Osgood, for she died nine months later on April 19, 1864. Andrew's father filed with the Federal Government for his son's pension, which was $8.00 a month, stating that he had been dependent upon his son's labor on the farm. Tragedy continued to touch the family, with the financial failure of the farm. In 1888 several friends of Mr. Osgood pleaded with the government to increase the pension. The government increased the payment to $12.00 a month, but the stress of losing his son, wife, and property had taken its toll; George Osgood died February 14, 1901.

Private Andrew E. Osgood
Company H, 13th Vermont Infantry
Row A, #20

The 13th Vermont on July 3rd was positioned on Cemetery Ridge about 300 yards east of the Codori Farm buildings. As Pickett's Confederate Division advanced against the Union center, it became divided by the Codori buildings, so that one Brigade, Brig. General James Kemper's, crossed the Emmitsburg Road and passed east of the farm buildings. This exposed the right of Kemper's Brigade to the Union fire on Cemetery Ridge. The 13th Vermont advanced 45 yards to a line of fence rails and opened a murderous fire upon the exposed Brigade's right as it passed before them, obliquing to their left to strike the Union line at the Angle. The regiment, supported by other Vermont units, swung into Kemper's rear throwing it into confusion and taking many prisoners.

Private Andrew Osgood advanced with the regiment into Kemper's rear, firing as rapidly as he could, until a bullet struck him down. Osgood was from Cabot, Vermont, born November 14, 1842. He was tall for the period, being six feet, with blue eyes and raven black hair. He died of his wounds on July 7th.

Priv. Joseph Simmons, Co. C, 13th Vermont Infantry, buried in Row A, grave #22 in the Vermont section. Died July 14th from the wound he received the third day of the battle.

New Hampshire Plot

Lieutenant Edmund Dascomb
Company G, 2nd New Hampshire Infantry
Row A, #11

The 2nd New Hampshire was in the Brigade of Colonel George Burling of the Third Corps. During the fighting of July 2nd, the regiment was detached from the Brigade and rushed to the aid of the line fighting in the Peach Orchard. It advanced to the apex of the Orchard and kept up a galling fire on the advancing Confederate ranks. The two regiments on either side of the 2nd New Hampshire withdrew under the enemy's pressure, forcing the 2nd to likewise retire from its advanced position. Lieutenant Dascomb commanding Company G, was severely wounded in this action and was assisted to the rear. He was from the state's capital of Concord, 23 years of age. He had been wounded earlier in the war at Williamsburg, Virginia, but this second wound proved fatal. Lieutenant Dascomb died July 13th.

Private James Hawkins
Company I, 12th New Hampshire Infantry
Row A, #14

James Hawkins' home was Centre Harbor, New Hampshire. He enlisted in the 12th New Hampshire August 14, 1862 at the age of 21, listing his height as 5 feet, 11½ inches.

"The New Hampshire Mountaineers," as the regiment was called resisted the Confederate assault on July 2nd along the Emmitsburg Road in the yard of the Klingel House, until it, along with the Division, retired back to Cemetery Ridge. Hawkins died the next day of the wound he had received during the withdrawal.

Unknown of the 2nd New Hampshire
Row B, #7

The question is usually asked, how can you determine who is buried in a grave which is marked unknown? This unknown grave is a good example of the detective work that is involved.

When Samuel Weaver painstakingly searched each individual grave and body attempting identification during the reburials, he would list those objects found on the body as well as physical features of the soldier. His detailed record keeping helps in present day research in our attempt to identify the many unknowns in the Cemetery. It was determined by Mr. Weaver that this soldier was of the 2nd New Hampshire, possibly because of his uniform or that he was buried with other men of the same regiment. Weaver then wrote in his notebook, that this individual soldier had "red chin whiskers." This physical feature must have been strikingly apparent for Weaver to note this in his record book.

Lieut. Edmund Dascomb, 2nd New Hampshire. (2nd New Hampshire Regimental)

Priv. James Hawkins, 12th New Hampshire. (12th New Hampshire Regimental)

Now comes the task to use this fragment of information in an attempt to determine who rests in this grave. The 2nd New Hampshire sustained a loss of 22 killed and 22 mortally wounded, a total of 44 in the battle. Those 22 mortally wounded can be ruled out, since this body was definitely taken from off the battlefield not a hospital site. Of the 22 killed in action we can rule out five, since their graves are identified in the New Hampshire plot. We can probably rule out six more who held the rank of corporal, sergeant, lieutenant and captain. This unknown soldier with "red chin whiskers" was probably a private, since Weaver doesn't mention any stripes or other form of rank on the body. That leaves only 11 men of the 2nd New Hampshire that this solder could possibly be. To further narrow down the possibilities we travel to the National Archives in Washington, and search the military service files, which most often tells us the soldier's height, color of eyes, and hair; in this case "red hair." Needless to say our research doesn't always bring success. The identity of this soldier from New Hampshire with "red chin whiskers" is at present still unknown. But the search goes on.

Rhode Island Plot

Private Alfred Gardner   Private William Jones
1st Rhode Island Artillery Battery B
Row B, #3   Row B, #4

It was the afternoon of July 3rd, and shot and shell from the massed Confederate artillery was pounding the Union line on Cemetery Ridge, in the greatest cannonade of field artillery of the war. Lieutenant Frank Haskell related:

> "We thought that at the Second Bull Run, at the Antietam and at Fredericksburg . . . we had heard heavy cannonading; they were but holiday salutes compared with this. . . . The projectiles shriek long and sharp. They hiss, they scream, they growl, they sputter; all sounds of life and rage; and each has its different note, and all are discordant. We see the solid shot strike axle, or pole, or wheel, and the tough iron and heart of oak snap and fly like straws. And these shot and shells have no respect for men."[93]

Brown's 1st Rhode Island Battery B, positioned near the now famous "Copse of Trees," was receiving a full force of the artillery barrage. Alfred Gardner's job in the battery was to take the artillery round and insert it into the muzzle of the cannon, whereupon William Jones would use his rammer to push the projectile down the barrel. As these two men were doing this, a Confederate shell struck the muzzle

Priv. Alfred Gardner, 1st Rhode Island Battery B. (Regimental)

Priv. John Mahoney, alias William Jones, 1st Rhode Island Battery B. (Regimental)

and exploded. Jones was killed instantly with part of his head torn off, while Gardner's arm was almost separated from his shoulder. Gardner possessed a strong faith in God, and so lying on the ground he cried forth in joyous praise, "Glory to God! I am happy! Hallelujah!" Before he died he asked that his Bible be sent to his wife Adelia.

Alfred Gardner was called by his fellow comrades, "old man Gardner," due to the fact that he was 40 years of age when he enlisted August of 1862. Gardner's military service record says he was 5 feet, 8 inches tall, having gray eyes and brown hair. In reality Gardner did not come from Rhode Island, but was born in Swansea, Massachusetts and made his home in Fall River. Alfred and Adelia had three children Lillian (born May 11, 1854), Alfred Jr. (born June 27, 1856), and Margaret (born October 7, 1858). Adelia Gardner died May 1, 1907.

William Jones was born December 6, 1837, but not as William Jones. His real name was John Mahoney. He was the only son of Michael and Margaret Mahoney. His father died on April 15, 1844 at the young age of 27. Margaret remarried in Boston on November 18, 1845 to Charles Nott. John was almost eight years of age at this time.

We can only speculate on why in August 1862 at the age of 23 John ran away from home enlisting at Providence in the 1st Rhode Island Battery B under the alias "William Jones." Was he trying to break from a possessive mother, fleeing from an abusive step-father, or seeking his own life? Whatever the reason, the fact remains, he did not want to be traced by his family.

In February 1863, at Falmouth, Virginia, a boyhood friend, Sergeant W. A. McGinnis met John; (I) 'addressed him as John, shook hands with him. He informed (me) that he was no longer John Mahoney, but William Jones, . . . that not wishing his mother to know that he had enlisted."[94]

It is unfortunate that John rests under his alias rather than his true name. These two comrades lie in death as they served on the battlefield, side by side.

"The Gettysburg Gun" of Battery B, 1st Rhode Island, showing the dent in the barrel made by the explosion of the Confederate shell and the cannonball wedged at the muzzle which Gardner and Mahoney were attempting to load in the barrel.

It should be noted that the artillery piece that was struck, called "the Gettysburg Gun," is displayed in the State Capital building in Providence, with the cannon ball that the two men were ramming down the barrel, still lodged at it's muzzle.

Sergt. Ira Z. Bennett, 1st Rhode Island Battery B. (regimental)

Sergeant Ira Z. Bennett
Battery B, 1st Rhode Island Artillery
Row A, #1

On August 25th, 1862 Sergeant Ira Bennett enlisted in Company B, the 19th Maine. He would months later be detached from the 19th Maine and assigned to the Rhode Island Battery B. He was 32 years of age from Montville, Maine.

Lucinda and Ira were married on September 17, 1856. The family grew to three daughters, Mary (born September 14, 1857), Julia (born May 16, 1860), and Zela (born September 3, 1862, a few days after her father had enlisted). Sergeant Bennett was killed under the iron hail of the artillery bombardment of July 3rd, serving the guns of Brown's Battery.

Lucinda was now a widow and ill prepared to care for three small girls by herself. Maybe the loss and strain were too great for her to bear, because she died a year later, October 25, in Montville.[95]

Priv. John Greene, 1st Rhode Island Battery B, buried in Row A, grave #5 in the Rhode Island section. He died from a wound received July 3rd in his thigh, which resulted in the amputation of his leg.

Rev. Enoch Miller, 108th New York. (William Gladstone collection)

New York Plot

Rev. Enoch K. Miller
Company F, 108th New York Infantry
Row G, #98

Private Enoch Miller, 5 feet, 4½ inches tall, stood with the color guard of the 108th New York, positioned in Ziegler's Grove on July 3rd. While born January 16, 1840 in London, England, when he enlisted, he placed his residence as Rochester, and his occupation as a theological student. He was wounded at Gettysburg in the left lung and discharged from the regiment. By March 1864, he had re-enlisted in the 25th U.S. Colored Regiment as its Chaplain. He served the unit until December 1865.

After the war he married Fannie M. Jeffords on September 21, 1867, and pastored churches in Newport, Delaware and North East, Maryland. He died December 30, 1903 serving the Lord in a church at Long Green, Maryland.

Captain Jason K. Backus
Company E, 157th New York Infantry
Row G, #109

Jason Backus joined the 157th New York as 1st Lieutenant on September 19, 1862. He shortly rose to the rank of Captain of Company E. Captain Backus was age 25 from Hamilton, New York.

Coster's Brigade of the XI Corps was advanced the afternoon of July 1st through the town, taking position in a brick yard just off North Stratton Street. Their orders were to hold the Confederate attack in check long enough for the rest of the Union line to withdraw back to Cemetery Hill. It was a sacrificial mission. The 157th held the Brigade's right flank. It was quickly outflanked and driven in confusion back into Gettysburg's already crowded streets. Captain Backus was struck in the forehead and instantly killed. His body was carried to the nearby Almshouse and buried, then later reburied twice, first to the Evergreen Cemetery and finally to this grave in the New York plot.

Captain Backus must have been a prudent investor of his money, (he received $115. a month as a captain) for he left a sizeable amount of money to his family. In his will, he left $200. to each of his three sisters, a valuable piece of property in Kansas to his brother, and a little over $300. to his mother. He also specified in his will, that $400. be given to the young woman he was engaged to marry. But this story continues with a twist.

Captain Backus' father, Benjamin Backus and his mother, Julia Backus, both applied for their son's Federal pension. The parents had separated in 1848 on very unfriendly terms. What followed was a bitter ''custody battle'' over their dead son's pension. Both hired attorneys to argue their respective cases, and each threw verbal dirt at each other. The pension office settled the matter by denying both parents the pension.[96]

Sergeant William T. Ambler
Company D, 57th New York Infantry
Row E, #91

''Its with most painful feelings, that I inform you of the death of our beloved Willie. He was killed instantly at the battle of Gettysburg by a solid shot entering his right shoulder and passing through his left side. He was gallantly performing his duty & died as a soldier should die, beloved by those in command over him & by those he commanded. He was always prompt to do his duty & although he enlisted as a private, he had risen to fill the position of a Sergeant & was in a fair way of promotion. His company & officers sympathize with you in your loss and will always remember Willie as a true & fine soldier in the support of our glorious country. It will be a matter of great satisfaction to you, to know, that we took possession of his body and buried him in a soldier's grave in the presence of his cousin Lieutenant Meade of the 4th Michigan Vols.

''Willie had some money in his possession, but before we recovered his body, the enemy had taken it from his pockets. His watch & c (chain) I delivered to Lieutenant Meade, who will see that you get them. I would have written before, but this is the first opportunity that has offered. As soon as we reach camp, I shall arrange matters so that you can get pay, bounty, & pension.

''Hoping that you will meet your loss with Christian resignation & fortitude & that you may feel that Willie died in a good cause while protecting the stars and stripes.

Your Obedient Servant
O.F. Middlelin
Lieutenant commanding
57th Regt. N.Y.V.''

This letter, notifying of the death of her son, was received by Mary A. Ambler in South Salem, New York. Sergeant Ambler was only 18 when he was killed July 2nd at the edge of the Wheatfield. He was the eldest son of Thomas V. and Mary Ann Timson Ambler. His father had died November 17, 1851 at the young age of 28. His mother would live to be a grand age of 86, passing away on February 21, 1908. Sergeant Ambler had two younger brothers, Lewis age 17, Albert age 15, and a younger sister Harriet age 13.

Sergeant Ambler, teasing his sister on February 2, 1863 wrote ''I am glad to hear a little of your nonsense as you call it once in a while. I don't call it nonsense if you do. We have had quite a snow here to about 4 or 5 inches I think, but last night there came a warm rain and took it all off double quick. I would like to be home and have a snow-ball (fight) with you first-scale. I guess if you would let me make 5 or 6 snow-balls ahead I could stand you and Albert—yes and Lewis to for that matter, and make you all run.''[97]

The Amber's were a close knit, caring family. Their loss could only be measured with a multitude of tears.

Sergt. William T. Ambler, 57th New York. (Ambler family)

Private Charles Spiesberger
Company D, 140th New York Infantry
Row D, #84

Private Spiesberger was born in Germany. He enlisted in the 140th New York at Rochester August 26, 1862, at the age of 18. His military file in the National Archives says he had light hair, gray eyes, was 5 feet, 8 inches in height and a machinist. He was struck down along with his regimental commander, Colonel Patrick O'Rorke, as the regiment counter-attacked off the summit of Little Round Top the afternoon of July 2nd.

Priv. Charles Spiesberger, 140th New York. (Carolyn Sickelco, NPS)

Color Sergeant Maurice Buckingham
Company C, 104th New York Infantry
Row B, #123

The following story is so heart-wrenching that the account narrated by a nurse in Christ Lutheran Church must be fully shared.

"It is difficult to discriminate where all are so brave, yet the bravest was a young Englishmen, the color bearer of a New York regiment. He came to this country an orphan boy, was educated in our free schools, found friends who assisted him, and became prosperous in business, and when this foul rebellion endangered the liberties of our land, and the bells everywhere were calling together the sons of the republic, he felt that for a country which had afforded him home and happiness it was an honor and a privilege to suffer and to die. He volunteered with the hundreds of thousands of freemen, and carried the colors of his regiment through all the battles fought by the Army of the Potomac until now, unhurt. All this he told me in broken sentences, and added that 'there was one on whom all his hopes centered, who made life precious and desirable to him,' and much more of a similar import too sacred to relate.

"To her I wrote a letter, telling of his sad state, how he had fallen, bleeding and wounded; and at his request, added that though he had lost his leg, he was proud to tell her he had saved the regimental colors, and his own life, too, was still spared him, which was only made valuable by thoughts

Private John Cassidy
Company D, 108th New York Infantry
Row B, #98

In April 1863, Private John Cassidy wrote to his mother and sister:

" . . . I got a letter from Jamey not long ago. He said he was well then and liked soldiering first rate. He must like it better than I do. . . . "

John Cassidy was from Rochester, New York, enlisting in the 108th New York, July 1862 at the age of 24. He listed his occupation as a moulder. At Gettysburg July 3rd, Cassidy was struck in the breast by a musket bullet and killed, as the regiment swept from Ziegler's Grove to counter-assault the left flank of the advancing enemy column.[98]

Priv. John Cassidy, 108th New York. (Regimental)

of her. This was surely enough to make any true woman feel proud that over so noble a heart she alone held sway. His wound was doing remarkable well, and every day, while attending to his wants, I would ask him pleasantly about the answer to our letter, remarking, that perhaps it was too full of sweet words to be seen by a stranger.

"At last, I found that all my cheerful words failed to rouse him from the despondent mood into which he had fallen, and I discovered his great anxiety at not receiving an answer to his letter. I begged him to be patient, and explained that the mail had been interrupted by the recent raid, all of which failed to reassure him; and when, going to him the next morning, I saw lying beside him on his pillow a letter, directed by a lady's delicate hand, I felt all would be well. Yes, the letter was delicately directed, delicately written, and delicately worded—but its meaning was not to be misunderstood, it was a cool, calm regret that she could no longer be his; to which was added the fear that the loss of his limb might affect his prospects in life. He handed me the letter to read, with a look of fixed despair—buried his head in the pillow, and wept like a child. To him she had been the embodiment of all that was true and lovely; and while others had mothers, sisters, and friends, she was his all. The blow had been sudden, but sure. When he looked up again, his face bore the pallor of marble, and I saw there was no hope. All day long we gave him stimulants, and tried by words of sympathy to rouse him, but in vain; he lingered two days, when the silver cord was loosed and the golden bowl broken. He died, and his last words were, 'tell her I forgive her.' "[99]

Fellow battlefield guide Tim Smith is to be applauded, for through his diligent research, the soldier of this gripping story is now identified.

Maurice Buckingham was born in England in 1838. We do not know how or when his parents died, nor when as a boy he came to America. When the Civil War began, he was living in the Geneseo, New York area, working as a "mechanic." He enlisted in the Wadsworth Guards February 25, 1862, which became Company C of the 104th New York. Cited for gallantry, he was promoted to Color Sergeant on January 1, 1863.

During the fighting on Oak Ridge July 1st, every member of the 104th's color guard were either killed or wounded. Sergeant Buckingham was wounded twice, in the shoulder and his right thigh, while carrying one of the regimental colors. He was carried to Christ Lutheran Church on Chambersburg Street where his right leg was amputated at the hip. He died July 20th.

Tim Smith remarks that a "fitting epitaph" to Sergeant Buckingham is found in the Register of Deaths in the Descriptive Book of the 104th New York, which simply says, "Noble Boy."

Priv. Francis M. Griswold, Co. C, 44th New York Infantry, buried in Row D, grave #98 of the New York section. He was from Italy Hill, Yates County, N.Y. and was killed on the slope of Little Round Top July 2nd, when struck in the head by a musket ball.

Priv. John Allen, Company C, 140th New York Infantry. Possibly one of the youngest casualties of the battle. He listed his age when he enlisted at 16, but his mother claimed that he was much younger. Family lore claims that upon the news of her son's death at Gettysburg she had his letters read and reread to her every evening until her own death some years later. Row B, grave #132

Lt. Col. Max Thoman, 59th New York. "The Jack of Diamonds". (Collection of Robert Fair)

Lieutenant Colonel Max A. Thoman
59th New York Infantry
Row A, #70

"Boys, bury me on the field."

Resting in this grave is the highest ranking officer buried in the National Cemetery who was a fatality of the battle.

Lieutenant Colonel Max Thoman had by the age of 31 experienced more practical military schooling to lead men into combat than most regimental commanders of either army. He wrote to the Chief of Staff, Major General Daniel Butterfield requesting a brigade command on February 20, 1863, listing his many qualifications.

"I received a military education in the Lyceum of Hanover, Germany from 1845–1848. I served as Lieutenant and Adjutant of the 9 (th) Infantry and Jann's Corps in the 3 years war of Schieswig-Holstein against Danemark, 1848–1851 gaining the experience of 21 different engagements. I served in the English Foreign Legion in 1855 not actively in the field but assisted to form it. From 1856–1858, I resided Central America during Walker's Expedition (against Nicarauga) where I learned most valuable lessons about warfare in a southern or tropical climate. I have served in the present

war, since 19 months with my regiment (59th New York) and looking about me with a soldier's eye, I must admit that I have learned good many valuable information of which I nor military science ever have dreamed of before! I speak English, French, German, & Spanish."

Max Thoman joined the 59th New York as captain of Company C October 8, 1861. He rose in rank to become Lieutenant Colonel of the regiment on January 8, 1863. He had received an earlier shell wound at the battle of Antietam, September 17, 1862. During the fighting of July 2nd at Gettysburg, Lieutenant Colonel Thoman was struck by a shell fragment which fractured his right shoulder. He died of this wound on July 11th.

His men spoke highly of his character and fighting spirit, calling him "the Jack of Diamonds." "He never flinched when duty called. His sword was ever ready and his men were eager to follow their brave leader."[100]

Priv. George H. Atkin, 84th New York (USMHI)

Private George H. Atkin
Company D, 84th New York Infantry
Row A, #14

Private Atkin was from Brooklyn, New York. Shortly after the battle of Antietam, fought on September 17, 1862, he wrote to his mother, Mary Horner Atkin:

"I will tell you what I have seen of the war lately all the way from Frederick and in every church, stable, house was full of wounded men with legs and arms off and diiing (dying) and I have been on the battlefield and seen hundreds of dead rebels and dead Union men and some of them with their heads and arms and legs off and such black and swollen heads and faces and bodies that you never seen and don't you think that is enough to see."

Private Atkin was killed July 1st at the age of 22.[101]

Sergeant Amos Humiston
Company C, 154th New York Infantry
Row B, #14

While the Union forces of the First and Eleventh Corps retreated through the streets of Gettysburg the afternoon of July 1st, the small Brigade of Colonel Charles Coster was thrown forward in a vain attempt to stem the Confederate advance. It was soon overwhelmed with many of the men cut down in the streets and many more captured, 178 of the 154th New York were taken prisoner.

Sergt. Amos Humiston, 154th New York. (NPS)

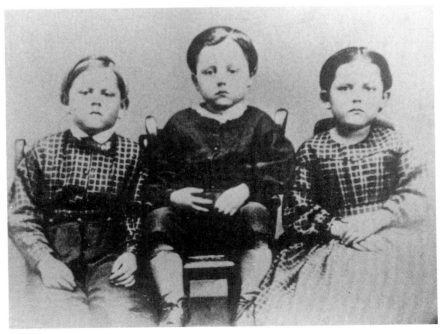

The Humiston children—Franklin, Fred, and Alice (NPS)

Near where the railroad tracks cross North Stratton Street, a sergeant of the 154th was struck in his chest just above his heart. Realizing that his life was quickly ebbing from him, he took from his pocket the ambrotype photograph of his three children. His last conscious thoughts were of his beloved little children.

After the battle, his body was discovered still clutching the photograph. No identification was found on his body, except that which revealed he was from the state of New York. The touching story of this devoted father made headlines in many northern papers. The photograph of the children was reproduced by the thousands and sold for .25¢ a copy, all the proceeds going into a fund for the widow and the children, which as yet had not been identified.

The photograph was widely published in several publications one being the American Presbyterian. The magazine was seen by Philinda Humiston of Portville, New York, who identified the three children as her own little ones. The soldier was Sergeant Amos Humiston. He was 32 years of age; born April 26, 1830, was 5 feet, 7 inches tall and a harness maker by trade.

"In early life he was a sailor and made several whaling voyages to the Southern Pacific. He was a man of noble, generous impulses, a quiet citizen, a kind neighbor and devotedly attached to his family. . . . He was anxious to enlist; but his duty to his family seemed then to be paramount to his duty to his country. But after the disastrous Peninsula campaign (Spring 1862) . . . and when he received assurance from responsible citizens that his family should be cared for during his absence, then without the prospect of a large bounty he enlisted as a private in Co. C, 154th N.Y.S.V."[102]

Philanda Humiston (courtesy of Mary Ruth Collins & Cindy A. Stauffer, "One Soldier's Legacy".)

His three children in the photograph were, Franklin age 8, (born April 10, 1855), Alice Eliza age 6 (born March 30, 1857), and Frederick age 4 (born January 17, 1859). Philinda Betsey Ensworth had been born in Norwick, New York on February 1, 1831. She had been married previously to Justin Smith of Hunt Hollow, New York (April 17, 1850), and had been widowed only a year later with the sudden death of her husband on January 10, 1851. Philinda and Amos Humiston were married in Candor, New York on July 14, 1854.

After the war, steps were taken to establish a National Orphanage for those children made fatherless by the war. In April 1866 it was decided to establish the school at Gettysburg. The structure chosen for the "Orphans' Homestead" still stands, located a few yards outside the eastern gate of the National Cemetery. Philinda Humiston was chosen as one of the first matrons of the orphanage and, with her three children, would reside within a few yards of where her husband is buried. Philinda would remarry on October 26, 1869 to Asa Barnes of Becket, Massachusetts and moved to that town with two of her children, Alice and Frederick. Franklin chose to stay and finish his schooling at the Gettysburg orphanage. Philinda would be widowed a third time when Asa Barnes died February 12, 1881.

By 1876 conditions at the Orphans' Homestead had taken a dire change from a secure loving home atmosphere to a place of fear and cruelty. The children had been repeatedly beaten, molested, and shackled in a dark dungeon in the cellar and treated like slaves. One boy had died. The matron, Mrs. Rosa Carmichael was arrested and convicted of aggravated assault against the students. She was fined $20. and ordered to leave town.

The Orphans' Homestead " . . . a very important endeavor fired by the traumatic fate of one Union soldier and the subsequent overwhelming sense of loss felt by his widow and three children, . . . " was closed in 1877. (To read more about the Orphans' Homestead, we recommend the booklet written by Mary Ruth Collins and Cindy A. Stauffer, "One Soldier's Legacy, The National Homestead at Gettysburg," published in 1993 by Thomas' Publications.)

Franklin, the eldest of the three Humiston children attended Dartmouth College and graduated from the University of Pennsylvania School of Medicine in 1886. He married Carrie Tarbell in 1886 and began his medical practice in Jaffrey, New Hampshire. He was the honored doctor of the community for 25 years, until his death on December 30, 1912.

Alice Humiston never married and worked in different fields; real estate, The Rhode Island Home and School for Dependent and Neglected Children in Providence and the New York State Department of Health in Albany. In the late 1920s she moved to Los Angeles, California, where she worked in the Library of U.C.L.A. She died December 1933 at the age of 76, from burns she received when her dress accidentally caught fire.

The youngest of the three children, Frederick, made his adult home in West Sommerville, Massachusetts, where he married Nettie Orne on September 17, 1896. He was a farmer and grain merchant in the area. He passed away on March 10, 1918.

Philinda Humiston, after the death of her third husband, lived with her son Franklin in Jaffrey, New Hampshire. She died there on November 18, 1913 at the grand age of 82.[103]

Michigan Plot

As you have probably noticed in your walk around the semicircular burial plots there are numerous mistakes on the headstones in regards to misspelled names and misidentified individuals. This is due to poor records and carelessness when the stones were carved in 1864–1865. The Michigan plot is a researcher's nightmare. There are at least 10 names of soldiers inscribed on the headstones who are not buried in those grave sites, nor are they even in this National Cemetery. Some examples are Private Albert S. Norris, 5th Michigan Cavalry, Row F, #12, who was wounded and captured at Gettysburg, but who died of pneumonia December 7th in a Richmond, Virginia Hospital. Sergeant Charles A. Ballard, Company E, 5th Michigan Cavalry whose name appears on the stone of Row D, #2. He received a wound in his right forearm, but did not die of this wound. He died at the ripe age of 88 on March 13, 1919 in Spanaway, Washington State where he is buried.

Also in the Michigan plot there are several duplicate engravings of names such as Private Artimus Clark, 5th Michigan Cavalry recorded as buried in Row D, #11, and Row I, #3. Lieutenant Gilbert A. Dickey, 24th Michigan Infantry is recorded in two graves; Row A, #7 and Row F, #15. Private William A. Cole's name, (5th Michigan Infantry) appears three times; Row B, #4, Row D, #14, Row I, #12. The correct grave site for Private Clark is Row D, #11, Lieutenant Dickey Row A, #7 and Private Cole, Row D, #14.

Private John G. Folkerts
Company B, 5th Michigan Infantry
Row D, #6

Colonel Regis de Trobriand, a brigade commander in the Third Corps, stated in his official battle report: "The unflinching bravery of the 5th Michigan, which sustained the loss of more than one half of its number without yielding a foot of ground, deserves to be especially mentioned here with due commendation."[104] The 5th Michigan fought July 2nd, on the western fringe of the Wheatfield upon a rocky spur, until forced to retire through a gauntlet of converging Confederate units.

Private John G. Folkerts was from Algonac, Michigan though originally from Hanover, Germany. He listed his occupation as a tailor, and his age as 45. Thus he was one of the oldest soldiers who was a casualty in the battle. He received a bullet in his lower right leg, shattering the bones. After the leg was amputated infection developed and he died September 5th.

He left behind in Michigan his wife, Jane, and four children: John G. Jr. age 13, Frederick J. age 4, Clare M. age 1 year, 8 months, and Martha 4 months of age. Mere words cannot describe the sorrow and emptiness that pervades a life when a loved one is lost in death, especially a violent death. Jane Folkert's sorrow and loss were too great for her to bear. Within a few months she was committed to an asylum, declared insane. She died 45 years later in the Eastern Michigan Asylum in Pontiac January 19, 1908.[105]

Corporal David C. Laird
Company A. 4th Michigan Infantry
Row B, #22

At the age of 19, David Laird had enlisted in the 4th Michigan, June 20, 1861. He was from Adrian, Michigan.

The 4th Michigan was involved in the ferocious seesaw fighting of the Wheatfield where the commander of the regiment, Colonel Harrison Jeffords received a mortal bayonet wound retrieving the regimental colors from enemy hands. The fighting was hand to hand. The 4th Michigan was driven from the bloody field. In their withdrawal, Corporal Laird was struck in the back, "the bullet entered (the) lumbar region one inch to the left of spinal column, passing downwards and forwards to the right side, fracturing . . . of 4th lumbar vertebra."[106]

In the weeks that followed the Rev. R.J. Parvin of the U.S. Christian Commission ministered to the young corporal. "We prayed, read and talked together, until at last the Spirit took possession of his heart."

Corporal Laird received the following letter from his mother.

"David, My Darling Boy: What can I say to you, my son! my son! Oh, that I could see you! that I could minister to you! I think father will probably be with you soon. My dear one, you have done what you could to suppress this cruel rebellion. May God comfort you! You are still serving the country so dear to your heart. You have been for thirty months an active volunteer; now you are a suffering one. Still there is an army in which you can enlist—the army of the Lord. All—all are welcome there. You will find kind friends who will keep us advised; and please request them to give us all the particulars of your situation. God comfort and sustain you, dear one, is your mother's prayer."[107]

Corporal Laird's father did arrive at his son's bed at Camp Letterman, but the young soldier's strength was failing. Corporal David Laird died in the early morning of September 24th.

Private James T. Bedell
Company F, 7th Michigan Cavalry
Row A, #23

Supposedly, Brig. General George A. Custer shouted, "Come on you Wolverines," as he led his Michigan Brigade in a magnificent cavalry charge against the oncoming Confederate horsemen the afternoon of July 3rd. The two opposing forces of cavalry crashed into each other in a wild melee of men and horses. Private James Bedell was unhorsed and taken prisoner. "He was hurried to the rear with other prisoners; in the subsequent retreat he was unable to keep up with the column, and all efforts to goad him on being unavailing, a Confederate lieutenant, in command of the provost guard, cut him down and left him for dead by the roadside. He was brought in by one of our scouting parties, and admitted to the Cavalry Corps hospital."[108]

For the next few weeks, Private Bedell wavered in and out of consciousness and rationality, "the tendency to stupor becoming greater and greater towards the close." He finally died near 5:00 p.m. on August 15th. The autopsy revealed that the sabre thrust had inflicted a cut six inches long in the skull, penetrating into Private Bedell's brain.

Private Bedell was a farmer from West Bloomfield, Michigan. He was 43 years of age when he died, or as some could say, was murdered.

The skull cap of Priv. James T. Bedell, showing the severity of the sabre thrust which mortally wounded him. (Armed Forces Institute of Pathology, Walter Reed Hospital, Washington, D.C.)

Maine Plot

Little Round Top has been termed the "key" to the defense of the Union line at Gettysburg. In regards to the saving of the hill (and thus the battle) for the Union army on July 2nd, several persons and regiments should receive credit: Brig. General G.K. Warren, Colonel Strong Vincent, Colonel Patrick O'Rorke of the 140th New York, the 44th New York, 83rd Pennsylvania, 16th Michigan and of course Colonel Joshua Lawrence Chamberlain and the men of the 20th Maine. The Mainers held the left flank of the Union line on the southern slope of Little Round Top. There they fought heroically, finally driving the Confederates off the slope by the point of the bayonet.

Sergeant Charles W. Steele
Company H, 20th Maine Infantry
Row E, #10

Sergeant Steele was from Wellfleet, Massachusetts, enlisting in the 20th Maine July 24, 1862 at Falmouth, Maine. He was 34 years of age and as so many of the members of the regiment, had been a farmer before the war.

During the savage close quarter fighting on the slope of Little Round Top, Sergeant Steele was critically wounded, "with a big hole in his chest." He staggered up to Captain Joseph Land of H Company. "I am going, Captain.", gasped Steele. "My God, Sergeant," cried the Captain as he attempted to catch him, but Steele collapsed dead at the Captain's feet.[109]

Private Orin Walker
Company K, 20th Maine Infantry
Row E, #4

The military files for Private Orin Walker records that he was 5 feet, 7 inches in height, having a dark complexion, blue eyes, and brown hair. He was 37 years of age when he enlisted at Portland, Maine on July 2, 1862. He was a carpenter by trade, living in the small Maine town of Norway with his wife, Salome Ann. (They were married June 27, 1848)

At Gettysburg, Company K was the third company from the right of the 20th Maine's regimental line on the slope of Little Round Top. The fire from the Confederate attacking ranks was murderous and without letup. Private Walker received a terrible wound. The huge soft lead bullet that struck him entered his left thigh passed upward then downward, tearing his intestines and scrotum and passing out on the right side of his anus. A wound of this severity was always fatal. In his agony, Private Walker was carried to the rear and made as comfortable as possible in his final moments of life.

But days, then weeks passed and Private Orin Walker still held onto life. He refused to give up and die. Slowly his horrible wound healed. He returned to his wife and family in Norway, having beaten the odds and the demon called death. He lived for another 20 years, dying June 2, 1882.[110]

Therefore, who is buried in this grave which is marked as Orin Walker? Definitely not Orin Walker. "Unknown—except to God."

Corporal Joseph D. Simpson
Company A, 20th Maine Infantry
Row F, #2

Born of French parents, Joseph Bureau changed his name to Simpson when he moved to Waterville, Maine. There at the age of 25 he married Harriet Chelró on September 2, 1856. He worked as a laborer in the small town and witnessed the birth of his three children; George Henry (born August 25, 1857), Paulena (born December 19, 1859), and little David, born only five months (March 7, 1862) before his father went off to war enlisting in the 20th Maine August 22nd.

By the time of Gettysburg he had gained the rank of corporal in Company A. During the violent struggle on the Little Round Top, Corporal Simpson received a bullet in the neck. He died the next day and was buried near the Henry Beitler farm. When his body was disinterred several months later they discovered a gold ring, probably his wedding ring, on his body. This ring along with several hundred other articles found on the bodies of the soldiers (bibles, combs, pins, pipes, letters, coins, toothbrushes, watches, etc.) were collected, packed and lost in the void of a government warehouse.[111]

Sergeant William S. Jordan
Company G, 20th Maine Infantry
Row C, #13

From Bangor, Maine, William Jordan enlisted in the 2nd Maine on November 25, 1861 at the age of 17. He would turn 18 in exactly two months, born January 25, 1844. When he enlisted he signed up for a two year term of service. However when the regiment was mustered into Federal service, the mustering officer had only the authority to muster the men into three years of service. Some of the men of the regiment therefore signed the three year papers, while others had refused. When May of 1863 came, the men of the 2nd Maine were preparing to leave as their term was expiring, but 120 were not allowed to go home, due to the three year papers they had signed. Sergeant William Jordan was among this group termed the "2nd Maine Mutineers." These men protested in vain, and at bayonet point were transferred to the command of the 20th Maine, with orders for Colonel Chamberlain to shoot them if they gave him any trouble. Colonel Chamberlain knew he couldn't shoot fellow Mainers. He quickly defused the situation, removed the guard and promised to help them in their claim of unfairness in the enlistment papers. All but six of the men of the 2nd Maine, Sergeant Jordan included, joined the ranks of the 20th Maine.

Cpl. Joseph D. Simpson, 20th Maine. (Collection of Robert Fair)

During the bitter fighting on the slope of Little Round Top, Sergeant Jordan took a bullet in his left chest and lung. He was carried to the rear to the farmhouse of Michael Fiscel. There, several weeks later as he lay dying, he was approached by one of the workers with the U.S. Christian Commission who offered him some booklets to read.

"He reached out his feeble hand, and looking them over picked out one with the title 'Welcome to Jesus,' printed in gold on a purple cover, and whispered to me to place that on the window-sill before him, upright so that he could see those words without turning his head. I did so. . . . The last comforting message he had was, as I have reason to believe, the soul-cheering one, 'Welcome to Jesus.'

Sergeant William Jordan passed into his rest on the 24th of July.[112]

Delaware Plot

Units from the "Diamond State" numbered only two: the 1st and 2nd Delaware Infantry Regiments, about 485 men total. The two regiments suffered casualties of 77 an 84 respectively. The 2nd Delaware (Colonel John Brooke's Brigade) saw its hardest fighting in the Wheatfield and the rocky ridge beyond. The Colonel of the regiment, William Baily in his official report stated:

"The Regiment moved briskly and with regularity, crossing stone walls, fences and a morass in the face of a heavy fire of musketry. The enemy immediately in our front occupied a most advantageous position behind a ledge of rocks upon the brow of a hill. (Rose Ridge) At the foot of this hill the regiment opened fire upon the enemy, and advanced rapidly up the ascent, driving him from his position. . . . "[113]

Private Jacob Steitz
Company A, 2nd Delaware Infantry
Row B, #2

Jacob Steitz was 42 years of age when he enlisted June 12, 1861 in the 2nd Delaware. Jacob and his wife Catharine were married June 4, 1838, residing in Philadelphia and raising a family of four children: Louisa (born 1840), Lizzie (born 1843), Kate (born 1846). Their fourth child was born in 1853 and was proudly named Franklin Pierce Steitz after the President. However their fourth child was not a boy but another girl. We suppose Jacob was desperate for a boy, even if it was a girl.

Jacob was mortally wounded July 2nd near the Wheatfield, dying July 8th.

West Virginia Plot

The western section of Virginia held Union rather than succession sentiments. Therefore on June 20, 1863 this western section entered the Union, after splitting from the Confederacy. West Virginia became the 35th State. The National flags carried by Federal regiments at Gettysburg displayed 34 stars in the Union; the star of West Virginia having not yet been added to the flag. However a story relates that the flag carried into combat by the 7th West Virginia indeed had 35 stars. It is told that some enterprising members of the regiment had secretly cut out one of the stars from the 14th Indiana's flag and sewed it upon their flag. Maybe one or some of the men resting here in the West Virginia plot had perpetrated this act.

The 7th West Virginia saw action at Gettysburg the evening of July 2nd only a few yards from where you are now standing, on East Cemetery Hill. Two Confederate brigades of Louisiana and North Carolina regiments in the darkness had assaulted the hill, sweeping aside Union units at its base and surging up its slopes into Union batteries on the hill's crest. Fierce hand to hand fighting ensued, until Union reinforcements, the 7th West Virginia included, rushed forward, driving the Confederates from the Union batteries and back off the hill.

Private Theodore Stewart
Company C, 7th West Virginia Infantry
Row A, #4

Private Stewart enlisted in the regiment August 7, 1861 at Sistersville, Virginia. He had been wounded earlier in the war at Fredericksburg and now at Gettysburg he received a wound in the right leg and thigh. The surgeon examining his wound, wrote that the wound would heal, "and will produce no permanent disability." However the wound did produce a "permanent disability"—Private Stewart died the next day July 3rd, from hemorrhaging. He was 21.

Private George Berger
Company G, 7th West Virginia Infantry
Row A, #5

George Berger was from Woodfield, Ohio, enlisting in 1861 at the age of 33. His service file says that he was arrested November 1862, charged with desertion and imprisoned in Fort Delaware, which is just south of Wilmington, on the Delaware River. The charge was soon dropped when evidence and testimony revealed that he was only traveling from a hospital to rejoin his regiment. Private Berger was killed in action on East Cemetery Hill the evening of July 2nd.

Illinois Plot

Private Charles W. Miner
Company C, 70th New York Infantry
Row A, #3

A bizarre story of coincidence comes from this grave site. Even though Private Miner was from the state of Illinois, he had enlisted in the 70th New York in the spring of 1861 because he was living with his grandparents in New York at the time. He was killed in action on July 2nd during the fighting along the Emmitsburg Road/Peach Orchard area. To understand the events that followed, we need to look back to when Private Miner was born.

In 1843 in the town of Lynn, Connecticut Charles B. Miner married Mary Smith. (This was his second marriage, his former wife, Eliza had died two years earlier.) Within a year the young bride gave birth to twin boys on February 15, 1844. The labor and birth were fatally difficult for her— in a few days she and one of the twins had died. The surviving baby boy was named Charles William Miner. As could be expected after losing two wives and one son in the short period of three years, the senior Charles Miner suffered a mental and physical breakdown. The new born baby was given to a neighbor, a Mrs. Otis, to be nursed. By mid 1845 Charles Miner had pulled his broken life back together and had even remarried, to Mary A. Taylor. They would retrieve the young Charles from the care of Mrs. Otis and the family began a new life, moving to Henry County, Illinois. Five more children would finally bless the Miner family, hopefully relieving some of the pain the father had endured.

But then came the Civil War, and Charles W. Miner, now age 19, would lose his life on the fields of Gettysburg. His father applied and received a pension from the Federal government because of his son's death. In 1883 at the age of 70, the senior Charles Miner passed away. His wife, Mary had the pension transferred to her name. But here arises the problem. You see, Mary Taylor Miner was of course not the natural mother of the soldier buried here, but the step-mother. "I took him though when an infant, one year old, and raised him, and he never knew any other mother," she testified. The pension office had taken it for granted that "Mary" (the step-mother) and "Mary" (the natural mother) were one and the same person. Mary Miner, the step-mother, was innocently ignorant to the fact that it was illegal for her to draw from her step-son's pension, but the Federal government didn't see it that way. By 1887 they had caught their error and had taken steps to reclaim their revenue. Mary Miner at this time, living near Sabetha, Kansas, was notified by the sheriff pounding on her door that she owed the government $365.47. She of course was shocked and being unable to pay the amount immediately, government agents seized part of her property as payment. The situation would be resolved in the courts, but sadly she had been unjustly maligned and mistreated by the government authorities.[114]

Corporal John Ackerman
Company K, 82nd Illinois Infantry
Row A, #5

The morning of July 2nd the 82nd Illinois was positioned on the western slope of Cemetery Hill. It had suffered the day before, nearly 100 men wounded and captured. In its present position on Cemetery Hill it was under intense and accurate fire from enemy sharpshooters barricaded in the houses on the town's outskirts. A detail from the 82nd was ordered "to dislodge the sharpshooters." The officer in command of this assault wrote of "an incident . . . which I shall surely remember as long as I live."

" . . . Brave John Ackerman, a private (Corporal) in my company, who on every previous occasion was the first to respond when volunteers were asked for to engage in some daring work, did not come to the front on this occasion. I was surprised at his action, and stepped over to speak to him about it. He said to me; 'Captain, I cannot go with you this time. I feel as though something terrible was going to happen to me today.' He looked pale and despondent. Believing that he did not feel well, I left him, after saying a few encouraging words to him. Within an hour after I left him, Ackerman was killed, a rebel shell cutting off more than half of his head."[115]

Corporal Ackerman could not escape his premonition. He was killed only a few yards from where he is buried. He was of the Jewish faith, age 27 from Chicago, Illinois.

Spanish-American War

There are four upright headstones in front of the Illinois plot that seem out of place. This is because these four soldiers were buried here years after the Civil War. Only one served during the Civil War, the others during the Spanish-American War (1898). In the Pennsylvania plot, Row G, #50 is another Spanish-American War veteran, Frank X. Weirick, Company M, 5th Pennsylvania, who died in 1902.

Private Jacob Noel
20th Illinois Infantry

Private Noel was drafted into the Federal service September 23, 1864 and served in the 20th Illinois until the unit was discharged and mustered out July 16, 1865. He died February 1900.

Private Harry S. Prager
2nd Tennessee Infantry

This soldier was from Dyersburg, Tennessee. His military file listed him as single, his age as 38 and his occupation as a blacksmith. He served in the Spanish-American War at Santiago, Cuba (July 1898), but was taken ill and transported to Camp Meade, Pennsylvania (near Harrisburg) where he died September 19, 1898.

Private Otto Kleinke
3rd Missouri Infantry

Kleinke enlisted at Jefferson Barracks, Missouri May 14, 1898. His service record says he was age 29, 5 feet, 5 inches in height, with blue eyes, brown hair, and a fair complexion. He listed his civilian occupation as a detective in Chicago, possibly with the Pinkerton Agency. He contracted typhoid and died August 25, 1898 at Camp Meade, Pennsylvania.

Private Other H. Thweatt
2nd Tennessee Infantry

A story of love, grief, poverty, and possible racial bigotry emerges from the grave of Other Thweatt. It begins shortly after the Civil War with Martha Rainey. She was a former mulatto slave of Indian blood, living in Todd County, Kentucky. After the war Martha, as their servant, lived with Mary Thweatt and her two bachelor sons, Tom and Peter. The elderly Mary Thweatt died and shortly afterwards the one son, Tom also died. By this time Martha and Peter Thweatt were deeply involved. Martha gave birth, possibly in 1875, to Other. Peter and Martha were not legally married, but continued to live together "as a family," moving to Nashville, Tennessee, where Peter purchased some property. Peter Thweatt died April 18, 1894, leaving a will in which he gave his entire estate to Martha and his son Other. Members of the Thweatt family contested the will on the grounds that Martha was not Peter's legal wife and that Other was therefore illegitimate. We would be remiss not to also mention that possibly another reason they contested the will was because of racial bigotry against Martha. After all the litigations and legal fees, Martha and Other received only $326.06 from the large estate. Martha said in a deposition that "they had robbed us of everything." Martha and her son afterwards lived in utter poverty, sleeping at times in a stable. To help his mother financially, Other joined the army on June 15, 1898. Within a few weeks he was hospitalized at City Hospital, Harrisburg, with Typhoid Fever, dying October 15, 1898.

So much had been taken from Martha: her dignity, her love, her home, and now her only child. She spent the rest of her life in poverty, laboring as a servant in different homes. She died, alone, January 9, 1921 and is buried in Nashville, Tennessee.[116]

Unknown Plots

There are three unknown sections, one we have already visited. In each of these unknown plots there are individuals who through today's research can be identified. It is so tragic that we know so little about these men, who are now just assigned a number.

Private Ole Thompson
Company B, 1st Minnesota Infantry
grave #71

Private Thompson was wounded in his left arm the early evening of July 2nd. His arm was amputated but he died of infection on August 14th.

Private John Morrison
Company H, 22nd Massachusetts Infantry
grave #255

Private Morrison was from Cambridge, Massachusetts, enlisting in the 22nd Regiment December 8, 1862 at the age of 29. His military file tells us that he was 5 feet, 10 inches in height, with blue eyes, brown hair, and a wheelwright by trade. He was killed July 2nd during the fighting in and around the Wheatfield.

Private Stephen J. Braddock
Battery C, 1st West Virginia Artillery
grave #260

Private Braddock was killed July 2nd, only a few yards from where he is buried. His battery is one of those gun positions you passed as you walked along the upper drive of the Cemetery. He was age 25 when he enlisted August 13, 1862, from Marletta, Ohio.

Private Isaac Vibbert
Company B, 3rd Indiana Cavalry
grave #261

Wounded during the cavalry action of July 1st, young Private Vibbert died two days later. He was from Harrison County, Indiana.

Private Henry O. Irwin
Company C, 80th New York Infantry
grave #280

He was age 22, and a laborer from Wawarsing, New York.

We have now completed the semicircular burial sections. Before you continue following the driveway, keeping the Evergreen Cemetery on your right, we would like to draw your attention briefly to this local cemetery. As you look beyond the iron fence into the Evergreen Cemetery, you will see a grave marker surmounted by a woman and an American flag flying beside it. This is the grave of the only Gettysburg civilian killed during the battle; Mary Virginia "Jennie" Wade.

Mary Virginia Wade, the only Gettysburg civilian killed during the battle. (NPS)

The grave of Mary Virginia Wade in the Evergreen Cemetery. The flag flies over her grave continuously.

Her sister, Georgia McClellan, had given birth to a son three days before the battle, therefore, Jennie, her mother, her 12 year old brother, and a neighbor boy, were in Georgia's house on Baltimore Street, just a few hundred yards from this spot. The house was literally on the front line, with skirmishers shooting from the upstairs windows. Bullets were striking the side of the house and an unexploded shell had crashed into the roof. Reason demanded that the family should have been in the shelter of the cellar, but Georgia was confined to bed and Jennie was in the kitchen preparing to bake bread on the morning of July 3rd. Suddenly a bullet, fired from the edge of town, splintered the outside door, bored through a second door that Jennie was standing behind, striking her in the back. She was killed instantly. She was originally buried behind the house, but now rests under the memorial in the local cemetery which was erected in 1901 by the Women's Relief Corps of the State of Iowa. The American flag over her grave is allowed to fly continuously.

The Evergreen Cemetery had originally been considered for the burial site of the Union dead. This plan was strongly opposed by David Wills, who had been appointed by Governor Curtin to establish a central burial site. Wills favored a separate Soldiers' National Cemetery controlled not by the local cemetery association, but by the eighteen states that contributed units to the battle.

After the battle there were numerous burials scattered over the fields and at the many hospitals. Mrs. Elizabeth Thorn, wife of the Evergreen caretaker, had buried within the cemetery grounds 91 soldiers. (Her husband, Peter Thorn, was in the Union Army and garrisoned at Harper's Ferry) Elizabeth Thorn was assisted in her ghoulish task by her elderly parents and her three young boys, she being six months pregnant.

Within time 27 of these bodies would be disinterred and laid to their final rest in the newly dedicated Soldiers' National Cemetery, leaving 64 still in a designated plot in the local cemetery. Two of these soldiers resting side by side are brothers. Corporal L.S. Greenlee, Company C, 140th Pennsylvania was killed in the Wheatfield area July 2nd. His brother Lieutenant Samuel Greenlee, Company F, 1st Pennsylvania Cavalry was killed in the battle of Hawe's Shop, Virginia, May 28, 1864. His body was brought to Gettysburg by their father on October 26, 1865, so the brothers could rest beside each other.

There are also two Confederate soldiers buried in the Evergreen Cemetery, Sergeant Matthew Goodson, 52nd North Carolina Regiment from Concord, North Carolina and Private Hooper Patrick Caffey, 3rd Alabama Regiment from Lowndesboro, Alabama. Their exact burial sites are unknown. In 1866 their bodies were discovered on the battlefield and buried within the local cemetery, but the outcry from the townsfolk forced the Cemetery Association to have the bodies removed outside the cemetery limits. As the years have passed the cemetery has grown in size, so that today these Confederate soldiers are now somewhere within the cemetery grounds. Two memorial stones have been erected in their honor.

The memorial stones for Sergt. Matthew Goodson, 52nd N.C. Inf. and Priv. Hooper Patrick Caffey, 3rd Alabama Inf. located in the Evergreen Cemetery.

The towering memorial on your left as you walk along the driveway is the New York State Memorial.

The New York Memorial, almost 50 feet in height, was erected in 1893. The female figure surmounting the column represents the State mourning her dead as she holds a wreath of flowers over the New York burial plot. Also inscribed on the memorial are the names of the officers from the state who were killed or mortally wounded during the battle. This memorial is the second largest monument on the battlefield; the Pennsylvania Memorial being the largest.

As you continue along the driveway, bending to the left around the curve, you will pass other monuments marking the positions of Union artillery: 5th New York Independent Battery, 1st Ohio Battery I. Also you will pass a small plaque erected in 1955 by the American Legion, which reads in part:

"The American Legion prays for peace,
but peace with honor."

We have now approached the eastern gate of the National Cemetery and the statue of Major General John F. Reynolds.

This statue, sculpted from melted cannon, was erected in 1872. The statue honors the highest ranking officer of either army to be killed in the Gettysburg battle; Major General John F. Reynolds. It was General Reynolds who led the Union First Corps onto the fields west of town during the early phase of battle, thus determining that the critical engagement of the war would be waged at Gettysburg. But within a few minutes General Reynolds was struck down. His loss was a severe blow to the Union cause, for he was ranked as one of the most courageous and capable of the general officers. He was deeply loved by his men and highly respected even by the enemy. There was also someone else who deeply loved John Reynolds, a person whom his family did not know about.

Two plots of unknown graves, with the New York State Memorial in the background.

Catherine Hewitt (Lancaster Historical Society)

Major General John F. Reynolds (LC)

John Fulton Reynolds was born September 20, 1820 in Lancaster, Pennsylvania and graduated from West Point in 1841, ranking 26th in a class of 52 cadets. He displayed conspicuous valor in the storming of Chapultepec Castle during the Mexican War, and was the Superintendent of Cadets at West Point when the Civil War began. But most of his military career was spent in the west. While in California he met a young woman, Catherine Hewitt, with whom he fell deeply in love.

Catherine Hewitt was originally from Oswego, New York, born April 1, 1839. She moved to California in 1856, shortly after the death of her parents and became a governess for a San Francisco family.

As the lifeless body of General Reynolds was being carried from the battlefield, members of his staff discovered a silver chain with a Catholic medal in the form of clasped hands attached, around the General's neck. Inscribed upon it were the words, "Dear Kate." Reynolds however was Protestant, and what added to the mystery was that his treasured West Point ring, which he normally wore around his neck, was missing. The general's body was transported to his sister's home in Philadelphia, where he lay in state. On the morning of July third, as the battle that Reynolds had initiated reached its climax, Catherine "Kate" Hewitt introduced herself to the general's family. She had in her possession the missing West Point ring. General Reynolds' sisters opened their hearts to Kate.

The General was laid to rest July 4th in Lancaster. A week later, Kate applied to Saint Joseph Central House of Sisters of Charity in Emmitsburg, Maryland, only 10 miles south of Gettysburg. One of General Reynolds' sisters wrote:

"Kate had his consent to enter a religious convent should she lose him, and now she intends to do it as the world has no interest for her now, she had given him first to God, then to his country, and then to herself. She said, 'to him I stand third.' "[117]

In 1865 Kate moved to Albany, New York and taught in a Sisters of Charity school. As the years passed, the Reynolds sisters kept in touch and reported in letters that Kate had developed a severe and persistent cough. It is believed that Kate had contacted tuberculosis. In September 1868 Kate left the school and the sisterhood and vanished. The story of General John Reynolds and Catherine Hewitt should not end this way, in a fog of uncertainty. If anyone has any information about Catherine Hewitt please contact the authors.

Continue around the curve of the drive walking back towards the Visitor's Center. The headstones on your immediate right are post Civil War graves. Some of these veterans participated in the Gettysburg battle, such as:

Rev. John Henry Wilburn Stuckenburg who was the Chaplain of the 145th Pennsylvania. After the war he pastored at different churches and taught at Gettysburg College. He died in London, England of a heart attack on May 28th, 1903, and his cremated body was shipped to Gettysburg for burial.

Lieutenant Colonel Willard Carpenter led the 4th Ohio Regiment in the evening counter-attack of East Cemetery Hill only a few hundred yards behind you. He died in 1910.

Captain Henry N. Minnigh who led Company K of the 30th Pennsylvania, "The boys who fought at home," in the Wheatfield the second day of the battle. He died on November 26, 1915.

Captain William E. Miller
Company H, 3rd Pennsylvania Calvary

You will notice a small government headstone written with gold leaf which signifies that this individual was awarded our country's highest decoration of valor; the Medal of Honor.

About three miles east of Gettysburg is a section of the battlefield that is seldom explored by the average visitor, East Cavalry Field. Over these rolling fields the afternoon of July 3rd was fought one of the largest cavalry engagements of the Civil War. Confederate cavalry, commanded by Major General JEB Stuart had attempted to swing into the Union rear, but collided with the Cavalry Division of Major General David Gregg reinforced by the cavalry brigade of the newly appointed Brig. General George A. Custer. The horsemen of both forces sparred against each other for several hours, until the Confederates emerged from the woodline in a magnificent classic cavalry charge. They galloped across the field of the Rummel Farm, to be met sabre for sabre by the charging horsemen of Custer's Michigan command.

Captain Miller commanded a squadron of the 3rd Pennsylvania Cavalry and had been ordered to hold his position on the Union right near the Low Dutch Road. But here was an opportunity to be seized. If he charged he could slice into the Confederate column which was sweeping in front of his squadron, but he had orders to hold his position, not to attack. Captain Miller turned to his friend Lieutenant Brooke-Rawle; "I have been ordered to hold this position, but if you will back me up in case I am court-martialed for disobedience, I will order a charge."[118] Lieutenant Brooke-Rawle consented, and the order was given. Captain Miller with his small detachment, "hit the (Confederate) column about the middle and cut his way clear through, cutting off a large portion and driving it back as far as Rummel's barn, although himself wounded (in the arm) and his horse killed."[119]

Capt. William E. Miller, 3rd Pa. Cav. Received the Medal of Honor for his actions at Gettysburg. (Regimental)

The headstone inscribed in gold leaf of Capt. William E. Miller.

81

For leading this gallant charge, Captain William Miller was awarded the Medal of Honor. After the war Captain Miller made his home in Carlisle, Pennsylvania, serving as the city's burgess and as a state senator. He died December 10, 1919.

Continuing along the drive back toward the western gate of the Cemetery, you will pass the graves of many other American men and women who have served our country during the Spanish-American War, the First and Second World Wars, the Korean War, the Vietnam Conflict and times of peace:

Albert J. Lentz, 18th Infantry Division, killed April 20, 1918 at Cantigney (World War I)

Charles A. Shuyler, Co. M, 145th Infantry, dying on November 4, 1918, seven days before World War I ended.

George Joseph Stembrosky, U.S. Navy killed during the Japanese attack on Pearl Harbor, December 7, 1941. (grave #198)

The Materewicz brothers, Frank (506th Infantry) and Edward (790th AAF Bomber Squadron) both killed during the Second World War, Edward on December 29, 1944 and Frank June 12, 1944. (graves #478 & #479)

Private Paul Heller, U.S. Marines, was killed on Guadalcanal, October 8, 1942 at the unbelievable age of 15, (born May 9, 1927) (grave #425)

Private Bernard Ulrich Stavely, 9th Marines, dying September 1, 1950 during the Korean War. (grave #2711)

Cpl. Robert E. Will, 814th Base Unit AAF (World War II), a dear friend and fellow battlefield guide who passed away November 2, 1973. (grave #11493)

Comm. Bruce W. Bugbee, U.S.N. a beloved friend who inspired so many in Gettysburg, dying July 20, 1994. (grave #61476)

1st Lieutenant Reginald Alfonso Stancil, Battery A 2nd Battalion, who was killed during the Tet Offensive in Vietnam on January 26, 1968 at the age of 19.

Beyond the stone wall to your right is the five acre National Cemetery Annex. Within this annex can be seen the impressive Friend to Friend Masonic Memorial sculptured by Ron Tunison and dedicated August 21, 1993. The memorial depicts mortally wounded Confederate Brig. General Lewis Armistead receiving aid from fellow freemason Union Captain Henry H. Bingham. This dramatic event occurred the afternoon of July 3rd on Cemetery Ridge, and "is only one of many documented events that transpired on the battlefield between Freemasons throughout the Civil War." It is urged that you take the time to examine this exceptionally beautiful memorial close up.

The Gettysburg National Cemetery is a living reminder of the high sacrifice, that at times must be paid to ensure the sacred treasure we call liberty. Although every day is worthy of a visit to these grounds, Memorial Day at Gettysburg is uniquely special. The Cemetery is decorated with over

Robert E. Will, 814th Army Air Force (Will family)

Albert J. Lentz, first man from Adams County, Pa. to die in the First World War. (Adams County Historical Society)

The Masonic Friend to Friend Memorial—Confederate General Lewis Armistead is seen here wounded and being assisted by a fellow member of the Masonic organization, Union Capt. Hiram Bigham. This unique bronze work is the only one at Gettysburg done in the poly-chrome patina process where chemicals are combined with the bronze to create a subtle hue of blue, gray and gold colors all of which are dependent upon the changing sunlight.

There are several symbolic objects on the monument: a fly portraying death and destruction, a butterfly the life after death where Armistead's soul would take flight, a cannonball signifies that the event occurred during the battle. Two bullets, one Union the other Confederate are also on the monument, representing that the two officers were on opposing sides.

7,000 American flags, one on every grave. The high-light of the Memorial Day services is the strewing of flowers by the children of the community over the graves. It is an emotional experience watching these future guardians of our country's liberty, pay homage to the guardians of the past.

As you leave the Gettysburg National Cemetery take with you not only the memory of those who rest here, but gratitude in your heart for what they sacrificed; and renewed dedication in your soul to what you can do to preserve our cherished national liberty. Remember, we are the guardians of the present.

Children of Gettysburg strewing flowers over the graves on Memorial Day.

PHOTOGRAPHS AND CIVIL WAR PHOTOGRAPHY

THE CARTE-DE-VISTE CAMERA- Shown here is a multi-lens camera invented by Frenchman Andre Disdéri in 1854. This model, equipped with four lenses, reduced costs by taking as many as eight images on a single photographic plate by masking a part of the plate so that one view at a time could be taken. The different lenses could record a range of views from full length to close-ups with the final product cut into separate pictures called carte-de-vistes. Desdéri became a wealthy man with his invention but squandered it all and died in poverty.

Although a small number of photographic images had been taken of the Mexican War in 1846 and the Crimean War of 1855, the American Civil War would be the first war in history in which a rich pictorial legacy was created. What made all of this possible was a series of European inventions and discoveries that took place less than thirty years prior to the American war.

The initial discovery, and where photography traces its roots, was the year 1837 when a professional Paris painter Louis Daguerre, by accident, discovered that he could record permanent images by using a solution of table salt and silver coated copper in a closed box or camera. The name he gave to the process was the daguerrotype. Two years later in 1839 the first daguerrotype was made in America and only a year later the world's first photography studio opened in New York City.

Early photographers could record still lifes and landscapes but not people because they could not remain still for the half-hour exposure time needed to record their image. Additionally, its commercial success suffered from the inability to make copies because no negative was created in the process. Another problem was insufficient light: Daguerre's crude lens simply did not concentrate enough of it. Immediately recognizing this problem and solving it in less than a year was Professor Josef Max Petval of the University of Vienna who designed an optical lens that multiplied camera light sixteen times. His "German Lens" soon became the world standard.

Another crucial advancement followed in 1851 when the English sculptor Frederick Scott Archer invented the collodion or wet-plate process where a wet chemical solution applied to a glass plate could be made to record sharp images that could be "printed" upon paper. More importantly, the "speed" of the new process was twenty times faster than the daguerreotype method and with the German Lens the exposure time decreased from minutes to seconds—or less. The same year that the wet plate process was discovered, Sir David Brewster invented a stereoscope camera that recorded three dimensional images. "Stereo" equipment would be employed by Civil War cameramen to bring all of the horrors of war in "3D" to the length and breadth of the land. The stereo camera simply mimicked the operation of the human visual system by simultaneously recording two images upon two separate optical lenses separated, like the pupils of the human eye. Then, when these slightly differing images were mounted upon a card and viewed through a hand-held device called a stereoscope the illusion of a 3D image appeared. President Lincoln had stereoscopic photographs taken of himself and recognizing the public relations aspect of the new medium eventually had 105 different photographs taken of himself. These combined advancements soon made war photography a reality on the battlefields of America.

When the boys in blue and gray marched off to war in 1861 leaving loved ones behind, the now affordable infant art of photography allowed the lowest ranking private the opportunity to present a personal memento to those loved ones which in turn allows us today to search for, track down and share with you the history and heritage of images of ordinary Americans who were called upon to accomplish extraordinary deeds; and when 600,000 who marched off to the glory of war suddenly found themselves sinking into that giant abyss of smoke and flame of a living hell and did not return, all that some loved ones had as a memento of their existence was a tiny picture that would forever remain as a sacred icon. And why not? Did they not, like warriors in the Old Testament of ancient times willingly surrender their own life's blood and earthly existence in a great moral crusade? And could they have been and were they not instruments of a higher Providence?

Epilog

As we conclude this study of Lincoln and the men of the Gettysburg National Cemetery let us resolve to remember and preserve that noble legacy of those vast and furious events of 1863. That heritage, untarnished and unprofaned, is all a part of an endless chain of events of a mysterious Providence that has now come down to us and has made us a part of all that has been before and all that will come to be.

Remember too, that the total sacrifice of a man's life as described in these pages was a total loss not only unto himself but a total loss of a life to others too of whom it can be said of many that for the soldier it represented loved ones he would nevermore kiss, families he nevermore would see and laughing children who would never be.

Footnotes

1. Pennsylvania General Assembly, Select Committee Relative to the Soldiers' National Cemetery. Revised Report (Harrisburg, Pa., 1865) p. 7
2. Ibid., p. 141
3. Ibid., p. 167
4. Ibid., p. 149
5. Ibid., p. 8
6. Ibid., p. 167
7. Ibid., p. 168
8. Ibid., p. 168.
9. Library of Congress, Long Remembered: The Gettysburg Address in Facsimile. (Washington, D.C. 1963), p. 2
10. Kunhardt, Philip B., A New Birth of Freedom (Boston, 1983) p. 42.
11. Warren, Louis A., Lincoln's Gettysburg Declaration. (Fort Wayne, Indiana, 1964), p. 53.
12. Ibid., p. 54.
13. Andrews, Mary Raymond, Shipman, The Perfect Tribute. (New York, 1906), pp. 5–6
14. Means, David C., Gettysburg on the Eve of an Address. Speech delivered on the occasion of the 103rd Anniversary of the Dedication of the Cemetery at Gettysburg, November 19, 1966. (Gettysburg, Pa.) p. 6.
15. Ibid., pp. 2–3
16. Ibid., p. 3
17. Ibid., p. 2
18. Barton, William E., Lincoln at Gettysburg (Indianapolis, Indiana, 1930) pp. 60–61
19. Mearns, p. 8
20. Randall, J. G. Lincoln the President Vol. II, (New York, 1945) p. 308
21. Library, p. 6
22. Library of Congress. David Wills to John Nicolay, January 19, 1894.

23. Kunhardt, p. 121
24. Massachusetts Historical Society, Edward Everett at Gettysburg. (Meridan, Connecticut, 1963) p. 2
25. Kunhardt, p. 122.
26. Warren, p. 89
27. Massachusetts, p. 2
28. Everett, Edward, Address of Honorable Edward Everett at the Consecration of the National Cemetery at Gettysburg, 19th November, 1863 (Boston, Mass. 1864) pp. 29–82.
29. Van Doren Stern, Philip, The Life and Writings of Abraham Lincoln. (New York, 1942) p. 375
30. Sandburg, Carl, Abraham Lincoln: The War Years, Vol. II, (New York, 1939) p. 472
31. National Archives Patent Office. A personal letter of Samuel Weaver dated November 25, 1863. (Civil War Times, November, 1960) p. 10
32. Van Doren Stern, p. 331
33. Ibid., p. 67
34. Ibid., pp. 348, 362, 502 and 540.
35. Ibid., p. 657
36. Ibid., pp. 841–842
37. Samuel Weaver, Report of the Select Committee of the Soldiers' National Cemetery, Singerly & Myers State Printers Harrisburg, Pa. 1865. pp. 149–151.
38. Letter of Lieut. Mimmack, Pension file of Lieut. Silas Miller #40269-28717, National Archives, Washington, D.C.
39. Gregory Coco, "On the Blood Stained Field II," Thomas Publications, Gettysburg, Pa. 1989, p. 75. Pension file #182398-138951, National Archives.
40. Minnesota State Historical Society, St. Paul, Minnesota, letter of Stephen Miller.
41. George Barger pension file #162337-133634, #463116, National Archives.
42. Cyrus Hall pension file, #28903-17754, #49073-78344, National Archives.
43. William Martin pension file #35868-29293, #662781-517997, National Archives.
44. Philip Tracy pension file, #52215-34370, National Archives.
45. Major Thomas W. Higgins, Regimental 73rd Ohio.
46. Richard Enderlin, Medal of Honor file, National Archives.
47. Sergt. Austin Stearns, "Three Years with Co. K." p. 190
48. Michael O'Laughlin pension file, #42093-17478, National Archives.
49. Edwin Field pension file, #311791-326311, #440103, National Archives.
50. Ilib.
51. Ilib.
52. Sergt. Austin Stearns, "Three Years with Co. K.," p. 189.
53. John Fly pension file #41636, #54809-14189, National Archives.
54. Charles Trask pension file, #160308-120943, National Archives.
55. Letter to Abigail Danforth, William F. Benson, Exeter, N.H.
56. George Hazzard, "History of the 1st Minnesota," Gaithersburg, Md. 1987, p. 344.
57. Capt. Nathan Messick pension file, National Archives.
58. Richard Moe Wright, "The Last Full Measure," Henry Holt & Co., N.Y., 1993, p. 287.
59. Bassett, "From Bull Run to Bristow Station," St. Paul, North Central Publishing Co. 1962, pp. 32–33. Richard Moe Wright, "The Last Full Measure," pp. 293–294.
60. James Wright, "Story of Co. F," p. 616. Ilib. p. 294.
61. Ilib.
62. Philip Hamlin pension file #187703, National Archives.
63. Aaron Greenwald pension file, National Archives.
64. Bachelder Papers, Major Theodore Ellis to Bachelder Nov. 3, 1870. Moses Clement pension file, National Archives.
65. Report of the General Agent of the State of N.Y. Albany, Comstock & Cassidy Printers, 1864, p. 44. Gregory Coco, "Killed in Action" Thomas Publications, Gettysburg, Pa. 1992, p. 24. Daniel Purdy pension file #474267-304215.
66. "Dear Bet," the letters of Lieut. Sidney Carter, Horace Fraser Rudisill, Darlington Historical Society, S.C.
67. Ilib.
68. Ilib.
69. Ilib.
70. War of the Rebellion Official Records of the Union and Confederate Armies, Series I, Vol. XXVII Part I, p. 273.
71. Dear Bet, Letters of Lieut. Sidney Carter, Darlington Historical Society, S.C.
72. Lieut. Col. George Stevens pension file, National Archives.
73. Francis Wallar, Milwaukee Sunday Telegraph, July 28, 1883.
74. James Sullivan, Milwaukee Sunday Telegraph, Dec. 20, 1885.
75. Sophrania E. Bucklin "In Hospital and Camp" Philadelphia, Pa. John E. Potter & Co., 1869 p. 181. Gregory Coco, "Killed in Action" p. 14.
76. Elwood Christ, "The Struggle for the Bliss Farm at Gettysburg," Butternut & Blue, Baltimore, Md. 1993, p. 58.
77. Haines History of Co. F, 12th N.J. p. 98. Elwood Christ, "The Struggle for the Bliss Farm at Gettysburg," p. 63. George Adams pension file, #254297-259189.
78. James Bennett pension file, National Archives.
79. Deeds of Valor, Perrien-Keydel Co. Detroit, Mich. 1907, Vol. I pp. 112–113.
80. Obituary of New York Times, May 12, 1902, July 29, 1917.
81. Stephen Kelly pension file, National Archives.
82. William Beaumont pension file #37027-105125, National Archives.
83. Col. St Clair Mulholland, 116th Pa. Regimental, Philadelphia, F. McManus Jr. & Co. 1903, p. 138.
84. Charles Gardner pension file #243139-343122, National Archives.
85. Elizabeth S. M. Stewart "Reminiscences of the Gettysburg Hospital," Gregory Coco, "Killed in Ac-

tion,'' p. 19. Amos Sweet pension file #37771-25598, #178499-140116.

86. Confederate Roll of Honor, Medal of Honor Society.

87. Letters of Isaac Osborne, courtesy of family, Betty Hunger & Jane Randall.

88. William McGrew pension file, #16842-39486, National Archives.

89. Elijah Leech pension file, #837739-664576, #613463-444477, National Archives.

90. John McNutt pension file, #380569-274570, National Archives.

91. Joseph Ashley pension file, #61087-69682, National Archives.

92. Horatio G. Jones, ''To the Christian Soldiers & Sailors of the Union'' op cit. p. 169. Gregory Coco, ''Killed in Action,'' p. 111, William Doubleday pension file, #38526-25222, National Archives.

93. Lieut. Frank Haskell

94. Alfred Gardner pension file, National Archives. John H. Rhodes, ''The History of Battery B 1st R.I. Artillery'' Providence, R.I. 1894, p. 209. John Mahoney pension file, National Archives.

95. Ira Bennett pension file, #28476-16377, #82445-47249, National Archives.

96. Capt. Jason Backus pension file, #224590-240228, National Archives.

97. William Ambler pension file, #36237-39788, National Archives.

98. John Cassidy pension file, National Archives.

99. Hospital scenes after the Battle of Gettysburg by the Patriot Daughters of Lancaster, 1864, pp. 32–34.

100. Lieut-Col. Max Thoman pension files, National Archives. New York At Gettysburg p. 440.

101. George Atkin pension file, #223931-185340, National Archives.

102. Letter from Rev. Isaac G. Ogden written December 17, 1863, Star & Sentinel; One Soldiers Legacy the National Homestead at Gettysburg, Mary Ruth Collina & Cindy A. Stouffer, Thomas Publications, Gettysburg, Pa. 1993, p. 17.

103. Ilib.

104. OR report of Col. DeTrobriand, Series I Vol. XXVII Part I, p. 519.

105. John Folkerts pension file, National Archives.

106. David Laird military file, National Archives.

107. Horatio G. Jones, ''To the Christian Soldiers & Sailors of the Union,'' Philadelphia, Pa. Lippincott's Press 1868, p. 166. Gregory Coco ''Killed in Action,'' pp. 46–47.

108. Otis Historical Archives, National Museum of Health & Medicine, Walter Reed Hospital, Washington, D.C.

109. John J. Pullen, ''The 20th Maine,'' Premier Civil War Classics, Fawcett Publications, Greenwich, Conn. 1962, p. 131.

110. Orin Walker pension file, National Archives.

111. Joseph Simpson pension file #165275-122219, National Archives.

112. Horatio B. Hackett, ''Christian Memorials of the War,'' Boston, Mass. 1864, p. 125. Gregory Coco, ''Killed in Action'' p. 53–55.

113. OR, report of Col. Baily 2nd Delaware, Series I, Vol. XXVII, Part I, pp. 402–405.

114. Charles Miner pension file, #354782-238709, #310242, 221418, National Archives.

115. ''History of the Jews of Chicago,'' Ass. Licensed Battlefield Guides files, Gettysburg, Pa. Gregory Coco, ''Killed in Action'' p. 33.

116. Other H. Thwealt pension file, National Archives.

117. ''General Reynolds and 'Dear Kate,' '' Mary R. Maloney, American Heritage Dec. 1963 pp. 62–65. Lancaster Co. Historical Society, Lancaster, Pa.

118. William Miller Medal of Honor file, National Archives.

119. Capt. D. M. Gilmore, 3rd Pa. Cav. ''With Gen. Gregg at Gettysburg,'' The Gettysburg Papers, Dayton, Ohio 1978, p. 479.

Suggested reference: ''The Last Full Measure,'' John Busey & David Martin, Longstreet House, 1988.

Rev. Roy E. Frampton became a Civil War ''buff'' when he was nine. Moving to Gettysburg in 1968 after graduation he joined the illustrious ranks of the Licensed Battlefield Guides. In 1972 he accepted the Lord's call to enter the ministry, graduating in 1977 from Lancaster Bible College with a BS in Bible/Theology and Pastoral Studies. He has pastored and filled numerous church pulpits in several states. He also teaches social studies at Adams County Christian Academy, and is the father of two children. Through the years he has gained a reputation on the Civil War lecture circuit as an informative and humorous speaker. The Gettysburg National Cemetery has been his passionate study for many years, centering his study on the personal lives of the soldiers buried in the Cemetery. Many hours have been spent scrutinizing pension files, reading soldiers' letters and diaries in the National Archives and family collections. He also appeared in the television series Civil War Journal, ''Lincoln at Gettysburg''.

Other publications he has authored include; ''The Inscriptions and Locations of the Gettysburg Battlefield Memorials'', and ''Noble Pillars: the Medal of Honor Recipients of the Gettysburg Campaign''.

James Cole is a native of Gettysburg and is a direct descendant of Nicholas Codori over whose farm Pickett's Charge was made in 1863.

One of the patriotic traditions of his family has been a citizen's duty of service to one's country as seen in the fact that Jim is one of seven brothers all of whom have seen active duty service in the U.S. military and all of whom volunteered as teenagers. Jim joined the navy at the youthful age of seventeen and soon became a petty officer serving in a naval air squadron as an Aviation Electronics Technician attached to the Pacific Defense Command.

After his naval service he returned to his life long interest in history to obtain a degree in education and history from Mount Saint Mary's College.

Jim has had a number of positions involving history and travel including Tour Director of Tauck Tours, news correspondent and Cruise Lecturer of the Swedish-American Cruise Lines lecturing on countries and cultures around the world.

Currently he works as a research-historian, operates a sales business Cole and Company of Gettysburg and serves as a U.S. Park battlefield guide.

He is considered an expert on a subject almost totally unknown to professional historians: The Gettysburg civilians who became hostages of war following the southern defeat at Gettysburg. Recently he led the effort to bring about the first marker at Gettysburg related to this dark page of American Civil War history. Jim is also the founder and chairman of the Gettysburg Citizens Rights Committee and is a member of the American Legion and the Catholic War Veterans Association.

Among historical publications he has authored the work, ''For God and Country,'' is the co-author of ''The Gettysburg National Cemetery: A History and Guide'' as well as this publication.